ISO 9000

9000

QUALITY SYSTEM

EDITED BY
DEE METLER

**DEPARTMENT BY DEPARTMENT
IMPLEMENTATION FOR THE CERTIFICATION AUDIT**

JACK KANHOLM

AQA Co.
LOS ANGELES

ISBN 1-882711-04-1

AQA Co.
334 Crane Blvd.
Los Angeles, CA 90065
Phn: (213) 222 3600
Fax: (213) 222 5239

Printed in the United States of America

To Pia

CONTENTS

INTRODUCTION

This is the fourth book written by Jack Kanholm for the AQA Co. ISO 9000 series. The book is an in-depth analysis of ISO 9000 quality systems and the auditing practices developed by certification bodies and registered auditors. Every requirement of the ISO 9000 standard is discussed, regardless of how subtle or controversial it may be. The emphasis is on understanding the intent and meaning of the requirements, and on providing examples of practical implementation solutions.

This book focuses on the design and implementation rather than the documentation of a quality system. An excellent example of ISO 9000 quality system documentation is provided in the *ISO 9000 Documentation, A 20-Section Quality Manual and 27 Operational Procedures* book, written by Jack Kanholm and published by AQA Co. An ideal companion to this text, it provides examples of how the quality system elements discussed here can be documented.

This book is intended for executive and departmental managers, consultants, and quality system auditors. Managers and consultants will benefit from the unique way the book is organized. It takes a practical approach to implementing ISO 9000 and explains the requirements as they apply to departments, functions, and activities in a company, rather than following the 20 sections of the ISO 9000 standard.

This book is also very useful for newly registered auditors. Lead auditor courses teach auditing techniques, but may not explain the interpretation of the ISO 9000 standard.

As a result, many auditors feel uncertain about interpreting the boundaries of the standard and are unable to hold their ground in controversial borderline cases. This book discusses the considerations that support sound judgment and consistent responses.

This book is based on the final voting draft of the 1994 revision of the ISO 9000 series of standards. In this new revision the sectional numbering for both ISO 9001 and ISO 9002 is synchronized. Consequently, there is no need to distinguish between equivalent sections from both standards. In this book, a reference to ISO 9000 means that both ISO 9001 and 9002 are being referenced. Whenever a reference is made to only one of these standards or to ISO 9003 or 9004, the exact number of the standard is used.

The commercial viability of publishing and distributing this book depends on the copyright protection. If you need additional copies, please use the order form enclosed at the back of the book, or call the publisher.

GOOD LUCK WITH YOUR ISO 9000 IMPLEMENTATION PROJECT AND CERTIFICATION OF YOUR QUALITY SYSTEM !

Jack Kanholm

2 OBJECTIVES AND METHODS

Evaluation of potential benefits from ISO 9000 is complex

Many companies have not yet heard of ISO 9000 or do not believe that implementation of the standards is going to help them in any way. At the other extreme are those companies that, due to customer or market demand, risk losing business if they do not implement and certify an ISO 9000 quality system. If your company is in either of these two categories, you're lucky — the decision to implement or not to implement the ISO 9000 system has been made for you.

In all other cases the decision is not so simple. The benefits are not easy to quantify or even to categorize. The most commonly considered benefits are:

- immediate enhancement of company image and marketing expected from the ISO 9000 certification;

- medium-term expectation for improvement of product quality; and

- in the long run, the development of a modern quality management system that responds to the demands of the global market.

This difficult decision is not made easier by the lack of precise and reliable information on how well ISO 9000 performs in attaining these goals.

Decide and clearly define objectives

No matter how complex the decision-making process is, management must clearly communicate the decision. If the decision is to implement and certify the ISO 9000 quality system, the implementation phases and associated objectives should be clearly defined. Those responsible for developing and implementing the system should have no doubt about what goals must be achieved at each phase.

To provide a quality management system

If the primary objective is to provide a modern quality management system for designing and manufacturing quality products, and the ISO 9000 certification is a secondary consideration, the quality system implementation project will be long and complex. It may involve reorganizing the company, redefining functional responsibilities, and implementing other fundamental changes in the way the company operates.

To reduce rate of rejects

If the primary objective is to reduce the rate of rejects, there is no need to implement all of the quality system elements right away. The most efficient way to attain this objective would be to focus on those elements that are directly relevant — for example, process control and training.

To attain ISO 9000 certification

If the immediate goal is to attain ISO 9000 certification, the design and implementation of the quality system should not emphasize any specific elements of the system, but rather concentrate on including all of the ISO 9000 requirements and addressing them systematically. A certification audit is usually failed not because a particular element of the quality system is not developed to its full potential, but because there is a complete lack of documentation and/or implementation for a specific ISO 9000 requirement.

Certification is a legitimate short-term goal only if continuous improvement is intended

Attaining ISO 9000 certification is a legitimate short-term goal. For many companies the certificate is important, and for some it may even be imperative. There is nothing fraudulent about wanting to get certified as quickly as possible with minimum investment and effort, as long as it is just the first step and not the ultimate goal. Registrars and auditors distinguish between those companies that want the certificate but do not care about their quality system, and those companies that need the certificate quickly and apply for it at an early stage in the development of their quality system but are committed to maintaining and further developing the system after the certification.

Lack of long-term commitment is easy to detect

Systems that are developed for the sole purpose of certification are very easily recognized. As an auditor, I like to know as soon as possible if I am auditing a real quality system or a patchwork of measures that are designed and implemented to pass for one. Whenever I see a company engage in arcane and unnecessary administrative routines that have no real objectives, I know that they were implemented to impress the auditors. An auditor is more impressed with a training procedure that clearly defines how training needs are identified than with a procedure that explains how to use 10 different forms to establish a training record. It is alarming to see elaborate traceability schemes compromised by mixing reworked components into batches that happen to be nearby. I am skeptical of the motivation for establishing a labeling scheme when the labels are not adequately attached and may end up on the floor. But most revealing are the activities of internal auditing and corrective actions. If there is no serious commitment to identify and correct problems, it means that the quality system was never meant to live beyond the certification audit.

Genuine commitment results in a more favorable audit

Naturally, auditors will assess a genuine quality system more favorably. When it is clear that the company is committed to work with and improve the system, some potentially major noncompliances will often be downgraded to minor and many minor noncompliances will not even be noted. Maintenance of the certification is also easier. Most registrars liberally apply the principle of benefit of doubt at the initial audit, but in subsequent follow-up audits are much less lenient with nonfunctioning systems.

Implementation should be guided by ISO 9000 requirements

When certification is the primary immediate goal, the design and implementation of the quality system should be guided by the ISO 9000 requirements rather than the need to find solutions to existing quality problems. The approach should be to document and implement every requirement on the system level with minimum detail regarding the specific techniques. With this approach, complex and in-depth procedures addressing selected problems should be avoided. The quality system, established on these principles, will be the least bureaucratic and obtrusive system that is certifiable.

Eliminates unnecessary elements in system

One of the many advantages to this approach is that nothing in the quality system will be unnecessary. If a company wants to be certified, it must address all ISO 9000 requirements regardless of its perceived needs, but they can be addressed primarily on the system level with minimum detail. The certificate can then be obtained relatively quickly without any waste of time, effort, and money.

System will be balanced and complete

Another advantage is that the quality system will be complete and well balanced, and thus be capable of working as a system rather than just an aggregate of detailed task-oriented procedures. In this initial phase the system will focus on the necessary organization: functional responsibilities, channels of communication, procedures for collecting and analyzing quality performance data, and mechanisms for requesting and implementing corrective actions. Once the framework is established, the system itself will determine how detailed and specific the departmental procedures and work instructions ought to be. If there are quality problems in any particular area, that can be identified by product verification and/or internal auditing programs, the corrective action might very well be to establish additional procedures, work instructions, training programs, etc.

Do not try to address specific problems before implementation

Quality managers often discriminate against those ISO 9000 requirements that do not seem to directly address existing quality problems. Most of the requirements seem irrelevant because the value of management reviews, contract reviews, internal audits, corrective actions, document control, inspection status identification, documented quality plans, etc., is not appreciated since these elements do not provide any *immediate* fixes. With this attitude, many of the ISO 9000 elements are likely to be poorly understood and inadequately developed.

Have confidence that every element will benefit the company

The successful implementation will accept the premise that the whole ISO 9000 is good for the company, even if it is not immediately apparent how some of the elements will work. Each and every requirement should be implemented based on a balanced approach to the details and without trying to fix existing problems. This philosophy dismisses the prejudice of irrelevance, and gives every element in the quality system the chance to be developed properly and integrated into a company-wide quality management system. Specific problems can be addressed only when a balanced and integrated system is in place. In fact, by virtue of the system's mechanisms, this will happen automatically.

Commit, design, document, and implement the quality system

This is one of those rare situations where doing it right is faster and cheaper, but it must be well planned. First, the management must have faith that when the system works as a whole, the results will follow. Then, someone must dedicate the necessary time to fully understand what the ISO 9000 standard requires and how these requirements should be interpreted in the context of the company. Next, the framework for the quality system should be designed and described in a quality manual and operational procedures. Finally, the departmental managers can be instructed to implement the operational procedures and, when appropriate, to supplement them with departmental procedures and work instructions. If the managers disagree with the operational procedures, they should request revisions, using the channels designated by the new system.

Internally audit the quality system and issue corrective actions

Shortly after the release of the operational procedures, the quality manager should start intense internal auditing and issue noncompliances and corrective action requests whenever he or she feels that full compliance with ISO 9000 is not achieved. At this stage, the corrective actions will in fact be the actions necessary to complete the development of the quality system required for certification. The noncompliances can at first be expressed in general terms to provoke corrective actions that require the establishment of departmental procedures and local subsystems. During subsequent auditing cycles, the noncompliances can gradually be more specific and pertain to particular problems with the implementation of these new procedures.

Use the system to complete the development cycle

This approach is a way to develop the quality system by using the system itself. The company's preparation for certification becomes an accelerated phase of quality system improvement rather than implementation of a fully developed ready-made system. This approach assures that the framework of the system is carefully designed by knowledgeable and motivated people without unqualified input from those who do not understand the requirements and the ultimate objectives. At the same time, it allows everyone to propose solutions that address the policies and requirements in their areas of jurisdiction. The key to the effectiveness of this approach is that the implementation, start-up, and building onto the quality system are done simultaneously.

 # MANAGEMENT

ISO 9000 quality system is a company-wide management system

ISO 9000 is different from other quality system models in that it is a management system regulating all activities of a company, from marketing to after-sale servicing. The only exception is accounting activities; even this will change, however, when the standard introduces requirements for quality cost accounting. This is not simply quality control — it is a company-wide management system. Active participation by executive and middle management is critical to the success of establishing and operating the quality system.

Executive management's role

Of course, there will always be organizations that look at ISO 9000 as yet another administrative requirement imposed on their companies by bureaucratic customers, regulatory agencies, or protectionistic Europe. However, unless the organization's management understands what is required and engages itself in the process, either the implementation of the new quality system will cost too much or company will fail the certification audit — or both.

Executive management's responsibilities

ISO 9000 Section 4.1, Management responsibilities, addresses the role and responsibilities of executive management. Specifically, the management will:

- define the quality policy;
- provide the required organization and resources, and define the responsibilities and authorities of personnel involved with the quality system;
- appoint the management representative for ISO 9000; and
- conduct management reviews of the quality system.

In addition, although not mentioned in the standard, management has an important role to play during the initial phase of establishing and implementing the quality system. The success of the implementation project will depend on a demonstrative expression of management support and the allocation of qualified resources.

QUALITY POLICY

Formulate
the policy

The chairman, the president, or a management committee must formulate the quality policy. Usually it is a 25-word sentence or two stating in one way or another that customer satisfaction is the point of reference for anything the company does. The *ISO 9000 Documentation* book contains an example of a quality policy. Another popular format is a list of 5 to 10 specific objectives naming customer needs, fitness for use, reliability, on-time delivery, and so forth. The content and format of the policy is never challenged by the certification auditors. The only enforceable requirement is that it must exist.

Document and
post the policy

The quality policy is normally documented in the quality manual, where it is printed in bold type on one of the first pages and is signed by the executive manager who formulated it. In addition, it is customary to post the policy in conspicuous locations throughout the company, so that all personnel can familiarize themselves with it, and it can be seen by the visiting customers and suppliers.

Implement
the policy

ISO 9000 Section 4.1.1 also requires that the policy be understood, implemented, and maintained at all levels of the company's organization. During the certification audit, the auditors may ask any employee what the quality policy is, how he or she understands it, and what he or she specifically does to implement it. ISO 9000 training should include presentation and discussion of the quality policy, and should explain how the quality system will attain the objectives of the policy (see Chapter 14).

ORGANIZATION

Develop the chart and list departmental responsibilities

The requirements of ISO 9000 Section 4.1.2, Organization, are basically satisfied by organizational charts and lists of responsibilities for each key management position. It is customary to include them in one of the first sections of the quality manual. In larger companies two organizational charts may be needed — one presenting the general organization of the whole company, and the other showing the internal organizations of the quality control and quality assurance departments. The responsibilities listed for each department need only be those that directly pertain to the quality system. The *ISO 9000 Documentation* book provides such a list of responsibilities in the first section of the quality manual.

Define the authority

ISO 9000 Section 4.1.2 also requires that the authorities and responsibilities of those having a role in the quality system be defined. This can be documented in job descriptions for the key personnel and/or in individual operational procedures dealing with specific elements of the quality system.

Assure consistency in titles and department names

Auditors will review the organizational charts very carefully, and will refer back to them frequently when reviewing the operational procedures. While this is not considered a noncompliance, it can cause confusion if, for example, the auditor reads about a production control unit but cannot find it in the organizational chart. The organizational charts should be made available to all personnel who write procedures to assure consistency in the use of management titles and names of departments, sections, and units.

Provide independent quality control and assurance functions

A more serious problem with some organizational charts is the lack of clarity in showing the paths of authority and, even worse, the lack of independence of the quality control and quality assurance functions. The typical symptom of this problem is the use of dotted lines. What does a dotted line mean? In some cases it has a legitimate use: to denote a path of authority that is valid only in special circumstances. If so, there should be a footnote with a definition or explanation.

But in most cases, dotted lines indicate that there is no clear path of authority. Auditors are skeptical when they see a solid line showing that the quality manager reports to the vice president of manufacturing operations and, in addition, a dotted line connecting the quality manager to the president. It probably means that normally the vice president of manufacturing operations is the quality manager's boss, except for the few days during the certification audit.

Must have authority to stop production and shipments

The question of independence of quality assurance comes up frequently. There is only one way to interpret the standard. ISO 9000 Section 4.1.2.1 lists five situations related to various quality functions where the concerned personnel must have the organizational freedom and authority to act in the interest of quality. Whatever the organization — big, small, traditional, or experimental — the bottom line is that there must be a person, independent of production, who is in charge of assuring quality; and he or she must have the authority to reject a delivery, stop the production, or hold back a shipment. Those responsible for identifying nonconforming products must have a direct and independent line of communication with this person. This should be clearly demonstrated on the organizational charts and in the procedures. Even though everything may look good in the documentation, auditors often investigate to verify that the authority is valid. The nonconforming product and corrective action records will provide the necessary evidence.

Independence is not in conflict with TQM

Companies operating a total quality management system (TQM) or quality circles and who, therefore, do not have independent quality control departments often complain that this requirement for organizational independence is in conflict with their systems. This is not necessarily the case. Production personnel can be responsible for inspections, identification of nonconforming products, initiation of corrective actions, and other quality functions; but they either must be vested with the authority to make final quality decisions (not very practical) or, they can report quality-related matters to those not responsible for the production output.

Production manager is excluded from the path of authority

For example, production personnel conducting inspections can report back to their direct supervisors who, in turn, either make the final decisions or report to the quality management representative (see next section) empowered with unlimited authority to stop receiving, production, and shipments. Thus, the person having the overall responsibility for production is not on this path of authority. Performance of the production personnel and supervisors in their quality verification functions can be checked by internal auditing, review of returned product statistics, or customer complaints.

Solutions for very small and very big companies

Other challenging situations are the cases of very small companies where an independent quality control department cannot be justified and, to the other extreme, large corporations with multiple product lines and production sites. The most practical solution for a small company is to designate the president or the owner management representative and vest him or her with the responsibility and authority to deal with all quality matters. Large corporations with multiple divisions and production plants normally have a corporate vice president or director for quality assurance, and quality managers for each division and/or plant. To comply with ISO 9000, every location must have a manager responsible for quality. Employees cannot be expected to use the telephone to report and resolve quality problems.

Most companies have traditional organizations

The cases of special management organizations, and very small and very large companies, are rare. The overwhelming majority of companies have traditional organizations: The quality assurance, quality engineering, and/or quality control department is managed by an independent vice president, director, or manager, who reports directly to the president, general director, or general manager.

MANAGEMENT REPRESENTATIVE

Designate
a representative
to enforce
ISO 9000

Just like any other regulatory authority, the International Organization for Standardization (ISO) and the registrars accredited to issue ISO 9000 certificates insist that there be a person responsible for enforcement of their regulations. They want to deal with a person designated explicitly to represent the company and empowered with adequate and defined authority to speak on the company's behalf.

The same is true for the customers. When they contract with or purchase from an ISO 9000 certified company, they want to know that there is a person responsible for the implementation and enforcement of quality requirements. This is considered to be an implied part of their contract.

Representative
reports quality
performance to
executive
management

Still another reason for the requirement to appoint a management representative is to make sure that there is someone in executive management that is involved with the quality system, and who can and will report on its performance to the other executive managers. To attain these objectives, the duties of the management representative must include taking responsibility for the implementation and enforcement of ISO 9000 requirements and representing the company in quality matters vis-à-vis certification bodies, regulatory bodies, and customers.

Representative
must have
authority

In most cases, companies appoint the quality assurance manager to be their management representative. This is an obvious choice. The quality manager is usually the best qualified and motivated person, and has the experience in establishing, implementing, and operating the quality system. However, a problem arises when the quality manager's role is limited to the management of product quality control without the authority to enforce other ISO 9000 requirements or to deal directly with external bodies. Possible solutions could be to elevate the authority of the quality manager, or appoint someone else to be the management representative, irrespective of his or her other responsibilities.

Appoint the representative and document his authority

Implementing the requirements of ISO 9000 Section 4.1.2.3, Management representative, is quite simple. It is sufficient to formally appoint the management representative and define the position's responsibility and authority. The appointment can be documented in the quality manual. The *ISO 9000 Documentation* book provides an example of such appointment in Section 1 of the Quality Manual.

MANAGEMENT REVIEW

More than audit assessment

Management reviews are often confused with reporting and assessing the results of internal quality audits. The 1987 version of the standard contained a note responsible for this confusion. The note was expressed in such complicated and convoluted language that most people could not understand what it meant. The phrase "assessment of the results of internal quality audits" was mentioned in the note, and it was natural to assume that this was the purpose of management reviews. In the 1994 version of the standard, the note disappeared. Section 4.1.3, Management review, is somewhat more specific. The results of internal audits are important and they should be assessed by management, but the purpose of management reviews is much broader.

Assess continuing suitability and effectiveness

The purpose of the reviews is to assess the continuing suitability and effectiveness of the quality system in reaching its objectives — implementation of the company's quality policy and compliance with the ISO 9000 requirements. Internal audit reports are critical inputs because they indicate how well the quality system is implemented and if it is effective. But other information is also required for the reviews, to include:

- Quality assurance should provide statistics on quality indicators, internal audit reports, and corrective and preventive actions;

- Marketing and sales should report how the markets react to the company's ISO 9000 certification and what it does to enhance the company's quality image; and

■ Production should supply data indicating how the quality system affects productivity; and so forth.

Based on this input, the management review deliberates and concludes if the quality system is suitable and effective in attaining its objectives and, if not, how the quality system should be improved.

A tool for controlling the quality system

In practice, the management review is the perfect tool for controlling and improving the quality system. Quality systems have the tendency to grow and develop a life of their own if they are not checked regularly. Whenever there is a problem or an audit noncompliance, the corrective actions invariably propose new and more complex procedures that do not necessarily improve quality or productivity. Management should encourage a quality system that is streamlined, intuitive, and understandable to everyone. Also, corrective actions should carefully address the root causes and propose effective solutions instead of needlessly building up the administrative aspects of the quality system.

Management meets at least once a year

To satisfy the requirements contained in ISO 9000 Section 4.1.3, Management review, the executive management should meet, or otherwise communicate, at least once a year to assess the quality system. A meeting is by far the most popular approach. When a company has multiple locations or there are other reasons why a meeting is not practical, other means of communication such as telephone, video conference, letters, memos, or reports are also acceptable.

The review body should represent various departments of the company, including marketing, sales, design, production, and quality assurance. A specific date, or at least the month of the year when the meeting will take place should be committed in advance. It is usual to synchronize the timing of management reviews with the completion of the internal auditing cycle and issuance of the final audit report.

During the early phases of the quality system — the first two years, for example — the management reviews should be scheduled more often, usually every six months. There should also be a provision for calling unscheduled management reviews to respond to unforeseen situations affecting the quality system.

Document the management review procedure

Once the format, participation, periodicity, and the objectives of the management review meetings are established, the whole procedure should be documented. This can be done either in the quality manual or, better yet, in a dedicated operational procedure. The procedure should also instruct how to establish a record of the review. It can be the minutes of the meeting or a written report with its findings and conclusions. An example of a management review procedure is included in the *ISO 9000 Documentation* book.

4 SALES DEPARTMENT

There are no direct requirements for quality in marketing!

Quality in marketing is not even mentioned in ISO 9001, 9002, or 9003; only ISO 9004 has a section dealing with it. But, as ISO 9000 certification does not require compliance with ISO 9004 — it is only a guide — it can be safely concluded that, at least for the purpose of certification, marketing does not need to be included in the quality system. Although this is a true statement, the lack of requirements for marketing is, in my opinion, a serious oversight.

How can the department that researches the customer's needs, defines the total product offering, and follows up with customer satisfaction surveys be excluded from the quality system? ISO 9000 has been strongly criticized for this shortcoming and it is very likely that some requirements for quality in marketing will be introduced in the future. But for now, this provides a slight reprieve for those companies that are focusing their attention on getting certified.

ISO 9000 requirements for the sales department

On the other hand, the requirements applicable to the sales department are quite explicit. They are contained in ISO 9000 Section 4.3, Contract review. In addition, like almost any other department, sales will need to comply with Section 4.5, Document and data control, and Section 4.16, Control of quality records. Although the requirements of contract review are relatively specific, their implementation will vary significantly from one company to another, depending on whether the products are standard catalog items or custom designs.

Standard catalog products vs custom products

The objectives — verification that the customer's requirements are adequately and clearly defined, and that the company can deliver what is required — are the same for both types of products. But the methods employed for verification of orders for standard catalog products often will be vastly different from the methods employed to review contracts for custom or customized products, especially when design is involved.

In the first case the focus is on checking that the ordered products are correctly and completely identified; that all other pertinent information related to packaging, shipping, and billing are included; and that the product is in stock and can be shipped by the requested date.

In the second case it is the customer that defines at least some aspects of the ordered product, and the contract review must determine if the stated requirements are sufficiently clear and complete so that there can be no doubt what the customer wants. The review must also assess if the company has the necessary means, resources, and time to design and manufacture the requested product. Because of these significant differences between the two cases, they will be discussed separately.

Customers often fail to adequately define their requirements

Logic would dictate that customers should know best what they want, and they usually do. But occasionally they do not accurately or completely define their requirements. A manufacturer that needs a new machine does not have to be an expert in machine design. While focusing on the performance characteristics, they may forget to state their requirements for reliability, serviceability, environmental compatibility, and so forth. Even customers who purchase standard catalog products often fail to adequately define their requirements. Illegible faxes, wrong part numbers, post office box shipping addresses, and all other imaginable mistakes and omissions on purchase orders are not uncommon.

STANDARD CATALOG PRODUCTS

Control incoming orders

The first concern is the system for receiving incoming orders. Personnel working in the mail room, the fax room, and operating the telephone switchboard should be instructed how to recognize orders and where to direct them. If the system for receiving orders is somewhat more complex, i.e. there are geographical divisions within the sales department or there are independent channels for processing orders for different kinds of products, spare parts, or servicing, auditors will expect some written procedures explaining how orders are segregated and routed to reach the correct sales unit. Once the orders are received at the locations where they will be processed, they should be logged or otherwise recorded, or placed in designated files or trays to prevent their misplacement or loss.

ISO 9000 does not contain any explicit requirements for receiving orders. However, the certification audit will invariably begin with how incoming orders are handled, and inadequate control at this point will make auditors skeptical of the whole order-processing system. The lack of documented procedures for receiving, routing, and recording orders will not lead to a noncompliance unless there is evidence that orders are being misplaced or lost. In most companies this is seldom a problem area whether the procedures are documented or not.

Review and verify customer requirements

The second concern is the verification that the ordered products are accurately and completely identified, and that all other pertinent information — relating to packaging, shipping, billing, and any other special requirements — are complete and understandable. Personnel should be provided with procedures explaining how to review orders. They must also have access to current reference information, such as product catalogs, price lists, shipping costs, and so forth. The procedures should stipulate what comprises a complete set of information necessary for each order, and what steps must be taken when errors, discrepancies, or ambiguities are identified.

Verify ability to deliver

The third concern is the verification that the ordered products are available and can be shipped to meet the requested delivery date. Auditors will focus their investigation on how the production scheduling information and/or the status of the finished products stock is communicated to sales. Usually, the status of stock is verified by using a computerized stock management system, a stock list, or stock cards. If lists or cards are used, the method and frequency of their updating and reconciliation should be specified.

When products are not stock and they must first be manufactured before they can be delivered, the system for verification and confirmation of the requested delivery date should require communication with production planning to ensure that the delivery dates accepted by sales are realistic.

Review does not need to be independent

The personnel appointed to carry out the order reviews do not need to be independent. The same person that enters orders into the computer, or otherwise processes them, can conduct the review. The process can also be automated. The order entry computer screens can be used to check the correctness and completeness of the data entered. Computer systems can be programmed to reject incorrect part numbers, prices, or zip codes, and refuse orders when products are out of stock. Whether the review is performed by the person entering the orders, his or her supervisor, or a computer program, the scope of the verification must be clearly defined. Following the verification, a record must be established evidencing that the verification was in fact carried out with a satisfactory result.

Establish record of review

The simplest contract review record is a sign-off or a stamp placed directly on the reviewed order, or on the form into which the order information was transferred. In computerized systems, the sales personnel entering orders may be required to type in their initials or otherwise identify themselves to evidence a successful order review. The manner of establishing the order review record must be described in a procedure. The storage location and retention period for these records must be also defined. It should be expected that certification auditors will examine the records to verify that the order reviews are conducted regularly and without exceptions. Missing sign-offs on purchase orders can result in a non-compliance.

Process verbal orders

Taking verbal orders, whether by telephone or at a walk-in order desk, is a special case. Here, auditors will expect that the sales personnel are provided with specially designed computer data entry screens or manual forms ensuring that the customers will be asked for all the necessary information. In addition to the standard information, the computer screens and forms must be adapted to accept special requirements, such as non-standard packaging, shipping, and billing instructions. Writing these instructions on margins or on separate notes will not be well received by auditors.

Confirm verbal orders

ISO 9000 also requires that verbal orders be confirmed. Confirmation can be written or verbal. To establish a verbal confirmation, the salesperson can repeat the order to the customer and ask for verbal confirmation. The verbal confirmation confirms that the order, as recorded, is indeed what the customer wanted. This method of verbal confirmation is often used by mail-order houses, airlines, hotels, and other businesses that take most of their orders by phone. A record of verbal confirmation can be established by the sales personnel typing in their identification (as discussed above for computerized order entry systems) or, even better, by giving the customer a confirmation number.

Auditors will verify the effectiveness of the order review system

Auditors will try to verify the effectiveness of the order review system by checking the history of product returns, back orders, and partial shipments, and by comparing the requested and accepted delivery dates with the actual shipping dates. If the history shows a pattern of returns, complaints, or partial and/or late shipping due to acceptance of incomplete or ambiguous purchase orders, or lack of verification of product availability, the auditors will consider not only a noncompliance relating to the order review system, but they will also investigate why the systems for internal auditing and corrective actions were not able to deal with these problems.

Therefore, if there is indeed a history of problems in this area, the internal audit reports should show that the problems have been identified and that corrective actions have been implemented, or at least have been requested. If this is the case, auditors not only may refrain from issuing a noncompliance, but they will be impressed with the company's concern for the effectiveness of their quality system and the system's ability to correct efficiency problems.

System for processing change orders

The last issue in this section is change orders. The relevant requirements are contained in ISO 9000 Section 4.3.3, Amendment to contract. The steps that need to be taken to process a change order — to include communication and interfacing with the design, production planning, production, and/or shipping departments, as appropriate — must be described in a procedure. In some cases it may be relevant to establish a formal system for handling change orders (comprising forms, authorizations, etc.) and to designate formal channels for interfacing with the customer and within the company.

A formal change order system will not be expected unless there is a high volume of change orders or the nature of the products (safety, importance, or value) warrants it. In most cases, a generalized procedure describing who reports what information to whom, how the change orders are reviewed, and what constitutes a record of the process is sufficient to comply with ISO 9000.

CUSTOMIZED PRODUCTS

Customized vs Custom design products

It is difficult to generalize for all custom products. Contract review will be vastly different if the product is a ship or a building than if it is a tabletop where the only custom feature is the specified dimensions. A practical way to approach this problem is to draw a line between those products that require only "standard" changes to an existing and proven design, and those that require a completely new engineering design. To distinguish between these two groups, I will refer to the first as customized products and to the second as custom design products.

Verify customer requirements for customized products

Review of orders for customized products can be handled in a way very similar to standard catalog products. There are, however, two differences. One is that the customized feature, a dimension, for example, is defined by the customer. The other is that the products cannot just be pulled from stock; they must be at least partially processed. The scope of order review must be adjusted to allow for these differences.

Personnel assigned to order verification must have the knowledge and/or access to information necessary to understand the special requirements, to assess if these requirements can be accommodated (technical feasibility, and capability,) and to estimate the time it will take to manufacture or customize the ordered products. Auditors will expect that either the sales personnel is competent in the relevant technical matters, or that the design or production department participates in the order review. In any case, production planning and sales should communicate regularly regarding the production scheduling.

Verify capacity to produce and deliver

Contract review for customized products is the most vulnerable to a noncompliance. It falls between the very simple case of standard products, for which it is easy to establish a straightforward review system, and the complex case of custom design products, where it is natural for many different departments of the company to participate in the review.

Although in theory the issues may be complex and interrelated, in practice there should be no problem as long as the scope of the contract review is complete; there is evidence of some kind of communication and interfacing regarding production capacity and scheduling; records of reviews are established regularly; and the review system is described in a procedure. Auditors will not investigate the competence of personnel or effectiveness of the whole system unless it is clear that it is not a legitimate system or there is evidence that it does not work.

CUSTOM DESIGN PRODUCTS

Verify customer requirements for custom design products

In the case of custom design products the difficulty is not so much with the implementation but rather with the documentation of the contract review system. Orders involving special design are never taken lightly. They often start with a written inquiry or invitation to bid, which is followed by a formal offer, and then there is a whole paper trail of correspondence, minutes of meetings, and other documents established during the contract negotiations. Nearly all of this documentation can be presented as evidence that the customer's requirements were analyzed and verified.

Verify capacity to design, produce, and deliver

As a rule, the capacity to design and deliver the ordered products is reviewed internally, usually at the stage of submitting the offer. The relevant documentation includes evidence that the customer's requirements were discussed and that the design and production departments confirmed the capacity to design and deliver on time.

Faced with such overwhelming documentation, auditors find it difficult to question the implementation of the design review requirement, even when they feel that the documents do not provide convincing evidence that there was a planned and methodical contract review. Arguing the point would require in-depth investigation and analysis of all documents, and there is no time for this during a certification audit.

On the other hand, establishing a contract review procedure for custom design products is difficult because the process is not always the same for each contract. Factors include the size of the contract, the manner in which the customer states requirements, and whether it is an old or a new customer. To accommodate this wide spec-

Establish contract review documentation

trum of possibilities, the contract review procedure should focus on what is applicable in every case; usually an offer and a contract, and the managers who negotiate with customers and are responsible for carrying out the contract work. Invariably this procedure will be rather general or even vague. But this is expected and the procedure will not be questioned as long as it identifies the managers responsible for conducting the review, and specifies what constitutes the contract review record. The *ISO 9000 Documentation* book contains an example of a contract review procedure.

System for processing change orders

The system for processing change orders for custom products is more vulnerable to noncompliances than the system for the initial contract review. One reason is that the change order processing system is often inadequately documented (insufficient scope of procedures), and the other reason is that it is much easier to audit. Change orders were already discussed in this chapter at the end of the section dealing with standard catalog products. The same principles apply, although here the process is more complicated because design and production are also involved.

The most common problem with change order procedures is that they focus on dealing with the customer on the commercial level and don't give sufficient attention to the technical review. Change orders should be reviewed to ensure that the customer's requirements are well understood and that the company has the capacity to implement them. Thus, the purpose and scope of the review are the same as for the initial order review. The procedure should define the scope of the review, instruct how to establish a record of the review, and identify the channels for communication between the concerned departments within the company.

Auditing the change order control system is relatively easy. The files are usually full of change orders that can be examined and compared against each other and the governing procedures. Implementing changes before change orders are formally issued is a common non-

Do not implement changes before change orders are formally approved

compliance. This often happens because agreement on cost increase and time extension cannot be reached in a timely manner and implementation of changes cannot wait. If this is the case, there should be a parallel system for approval of change orders for technical content only. Unauthorized implementation of changes cannot be accepted, even though there may be full confidence that the corresponding change orders will be formally executed at a later time.

5 DESIGN DEPARTMENT

The most serious noncompliances are found in design control

Statistics compiled by ISO 9000 certification bodies consistently show that design control is the area where most serious noncompliances are found. Among the most common reasons are:

- lack of understanding of the requirements;
- difficulty in conceptualizing how a quality system should work in design;
- unwillingness of engineers to submit to a system;
- inadequate authority of the QA manager over the design department.

All of these reasons result from lack of experience with the application of quality assurance in design. ISO 9000 is one of the first general quality system standards that includes design activities.

9001 vs 9002

The visibility of the design department is further increased by the unique position of design control in the ISO 9000 standards. Section 4.4, Design control, of ISO 9001 does not exist in 9002, and this is the only major difference between the two standards. The distinction between being certified for ISO 9001 and 9002 is the implementation of quality assurance in design. Naturally, auditors are careful to make certain that there is substance behind this distinction. It is an unwritten rule that the lead auditor audits the design department personally to verify that the ISO 9001 certificate is well deserved.

My personal experience as an auditor and a consultant concurs with the statistics and the difficulties in understanding what is required. The design department is

30 ISO 9000 QUALITY SYSTEM

More than
control of
drawings

usually the last to write its procedures and to start implementation of the system. In their procedures, engineers often focus on the management and control of drawings, specifications, and other design output documents, but they usually neglect to address the principal requirements of Section 4.4, namely those pertaining to control of the design itself. Quality assurance departments accept this incomplete system because they generally don't have sufficient knowledge of the design process and they lack the authority to impose any requirements on the design department. This is a classic scenario for failing the certification audit.

THE PRINCIPLES

How can
quality system
be applied to
design activities?

The root problem in understanding how quality assurance should be applied to design activities lies in the way most design departments operate. Engineers are the educated individualists that carry most of their knowledge in their heads and the rest is locked up in their private desk drawers. Planning? Sure. There is one long line on the job schedule showing the duration of the design phase. Activity assignment? Of course. Everybody knows that Bill always does the structural and Jim the electrical. Interfacing? No problem. Bill and Jim sit two desks away from each other and both speak English. Verification of input requirements? Hey, we know what these machines are for!....

The primary
product is not a
set of drawings,
but the design
itself

The key to applying quality assurance and to understanding the ISO 9000 requirements in design is to look at the design activities as production. The primary product is not (as many believe) a set of drawings and specifications, but the design itself. Drawings, specifications, and other related documents are only the embodiment of a design — a medium that communicates the design to others. Another important role of the design documents is that they instruct how to build the designed product. The ISO 9001 Section 4.4, Design control, is about the design process, of which the drawings and specifications are only the design output.

Customer of design can be external or internal

The design is initiated by a customer need or requirement. The customer can be internal, as when the marketing department wants to develop a new product, or the service department needs some parts redesigned to improve reliability; or it can be an external customer represented by the sales department. The concept of having a customer is important, but the concept is often lost when the customer is an internal department. When there is an external customer with specific requirements, there is a better chance that the requirements will be documented; the design process will focus on satisfying these requirements; and there will be reviews and verifications to determine if the design satisfies the stated requirements.

The design process defined

Few design projects experience the creative moment when an invention or a discovery is made, and therefore the design process remains just another form of production. First, the customer's requirements are compiled into design input data and are reviewed. Then the design project is planned and divided into phases and processes, and verifications are prescribed at certain stages, much like in-process inspections in manufacturing. Finally, when the design is completed, it is verified to determine if the design output meets the design input requirements. If the design is approved, it is formally released for production.

Design control is a "production" process

Looking at design activities through this "production" perspective, and remembering that the product is the design and not the drawings, is very helpful for applying quality assurance to design. Design input together with regulatory and other customary requirements are equivalent to production drawings and specifications. Reference materials (such as similar proven designs, research data, catalogs, textbooks, etc.) and the education and experience of engineers are the raw materials and components for the design. Computer programs, simulators, tests, experiments, and the mental processes of engineers are the equipment and processes used in production of the design. The drawings and specifications are design output which is the embodiment of the design product.

In this context it should be clear that:

- the design input must be reviewed and approved just as production drawings must be;
- the reference materials and qualifications of engineers must be of known quality just as raw materials and components must be;
- computer programs and design methods must be qualified just as production equipment and processes must be;
- and, at the end, the design must be verified, just as a product must be, to confirm that it satisfies the stated requirements.

In addition, there are the usual organizational controls, such as planning, scheduling, and assignment of activities.

DESIGN INPUT

Document customer requirements

A design project may be initiated by a request from another department to develop a new product or improve an existing one, by an order from an external customer, or in response to a tender. In some cases, all of the characteristics, performance, and other requirements for the product design are transmitted to the design department in one concise document. In other cases, definition of these requirements may be forthcoming over a long period of time because of lengthy consultations and negotiations. Even at the start of the design project, it may be that not all of the requirements have been fully defined. Whatever the format or stages of establishing and documenting the customer's requirements, they are the design input.

Collect and organize design input information

The information that defines the design input is often documented in a collection of faxes, letters, memos, and minutes of meetings. Design input can be expressed in a variety of forms, such as data, photographs, and references to other similar products. All pertinent information should be indexed, logged, or otherwise organized to make it readily accessible. If possible, it would be ideal if the information was interpreted and transcribed to a single standard document. The system for collecting and organizing the design input must allow for changes. When the customer comes back with a new or modified requirement, it is critical to identify which of the originally stated requirements become obsolete as a result of the change.

Review and approve design input

After the design input information is identified, documented, and organized, the design input should be reviewed for completeness, ambiguities, and conflicting requirements. Any problems should be resolved with the customer at this stage. When satisfactory, the design input should be formally released to the design or engineering department. When the information is forthcoming in stages or it is known in advance that the design will have to be started before all requirements are defined, the review process can also be carried out in stages. In this event, there should be a system for tracking which requirements have yet to be defined and what the deadlines are for defining them.

Establish the record of review and approval

The review and approval of design input must be recorded. Any reasonable format of the review record is acceptable. In the simplest case, when the order for design contains all of the necessary design information in one standard document (such as a purchase order) it is sufficient that the person responsible for review and approval of the design input initial and date the document. In more complex situations, the review can be recorded on a memo or a form that references the appropriate documents containing the design input information and states that these documents were reviewed and approved.

Establish procedure for design input

The procedure that deals with the design input should assign the responsibility for design input review and approval; and describe the process, which may include how the design input information is organized, unless it is obvious. The procedure should also instruct that only approved design input information can be used for the design, and should define how approved documents can be distinguished from those that carry only preliminary information.

DESIGN PLANNING

Design planning needs to be formalized

In a small company that may only have three engineers and two draftsmen in the design department, people shake their heads when they read about planning, activity assignment, and organizational interfaces in the ISO 9000 standard. They have been working without these things for the last 20 years and never felt they were missing anything. However, a closer examination reveals that, in fact, they are planning and interfacing, but there is no formal system. The individual design projects are identified by consecutive project numbers, the estimated time for completing the design is known, and there is a schedule of drawings that need to be established.

Compliance for the small company

Although the company may not be aware of it, this small design department is very close to achieving compliance with ISO 9000 Section 4.4.2, Design and development planning. All they need to do is establish a one-page chart at the start of a new project. The chart identifies all activities of the project (including verification), and schedules out and assigns personnel to each activity. For example, the first few activities may be:

ACTIVITY	INPUT	ASSIGNED	START	FINISH	VERIFY
Review and approval of design input	Purchase order from sales	John	07/15	07/18	Not applicable
Selection and calculation of speed, torque and other parameters	Design input from John	Alex	07/18	09/22	John
Selection and design of drive train	Loads and performance data from John	Thomas	07/21	09/29	John

And the last two entries might be:

ACTIVITY	INPUT	ASSIGNED	START	FINISH	VERIFY
General assembly drawing and bill of materials	All detail drawings	Isabel	09/11	09/19	Alex, Thomas and John
Design review meeting and release of design	All design output documents	Sales, Production, QA, Engineering	09/25	09/25	Not applicable

If the department always designs similar products and the main activities are the same, the chart can be preprinted so that only names and dates need to be written in. There could also be a "comment" column for recording the actual completion dates and reasons for delays.

For the small company, all that would be needed in the procedure dealing with design project organization is:

- an explanation of the purpose and use of the project planning chart;

- the assignment of responsibility for establishing and maintaining the chart; and

- designation of the location where the chart will kept during the project and where will it be filed after completion.

Complex designs require more extensive planning

Larger companies can use a similar chart if their design activities are equally as simple. When design is a complex process involving research, use of external consultants, prototype building, and extensive testing, a much more sophisticated organization system must be implemented. A fully developed system for management of complex design projects should comprise the following elements:

- critical path scheduling;

- project organization charts;

- document transmittal letters;
- tracking logs for receipt and transmittal of documents and information;
- schedules for releasing drawings, specifications, and other design output documentation;
- progress meetings and design review meetings.

For large and complex projects, the design project management system should be described in a separate procedure. It should explain how every element of the system works, what forms are used, who is responsible, and how documents are maintained and filed.

Example procedure for scheduling

Regarding scheduling, for example, the procedure could read: ".... Within the first two weeks after the start of a design project, the Project Chief Engineer establishes a project schedule. The schedule is a CPM type schedule. It shows all major phases of the project, such as preliminary design, model building, detail design, production of drawings, and prototype building and testing. Each phase is further broken down into activities, such as drafting, calculations, verifications, coordination meetings, and design review meetings. Interfacing and deadlines for transmitting key data between various design groups also are indicated on the schedule. The schedule is displayed on a wall in the Project Chief Engineer's office. Adherence to the schedule is assessed at weekly progress meetings. The schedule is revised or reissued when there is a serious delay or important change in design input. Completion dates for major design phases may not be changed without consent from either Marketing or Sales, depending on which department ordered the design..."

Simple or complex... requirements can still be satisfied

These two examples — a small company using a simple form to schedule and assign design activities, and a large and complex project that requires a fully developed design project management system — illustrate how the same set of requirements in ISO 9000 may have to be satisfied on extremely different levels depending on particular circumstances. In most companies, the applicable system will be somewhere in between. Regardless of the size and complexity, the cornerstones of any design control system that satisfies Section 4.4.2 are identification of design phases and activities (including verification), activity assignment, and a schedule.

Be prepared to provide the evidence of personnel qualifications

The final requirement of Section 4.4.2 is that design and verification activities be assigned to qualified personnel. During the certification audit, auditors are likely to ask for evidence that a specific person is qualified. A file containing professional resume, copies of diplomas, certificates from seminars, and records of in-house training will provide the evidence.

If the personnel qualification and training files are incomplete because, prior to implementation of ISO 9000, these documents were not collected and filed on a regular basis, those employees that have been with the company for a longer period of time (one year or more, for example) can be grandfathered. A certificate from their supervisor or manager stating that they have proven themselves to be adequately qualified by satisfactory on-the-job performance will evidence their qualifications.

REFERENCE MATERIALS

First impressions

Often the first things the auditor observes in the design department are the bookcases, shelves, and cabinets filled with catalogs, standards, textbooks, reports, magazines, manuals, computer printouts, unfinished drawings, and files on old projects. The material is often in a state of disarray, spilling out of shelves and towering in unstable piles on top of cabinets. Most likely there is more of the same in individual offices and work areas, and even the floor has been known to be used for document storage.

It is true that ISO 9000 does not require that reference materials be controlled (unless they are standards used in defining design input). Fair or not, however, a design department that resembles this description will have a hard time convincing an auditor that everything else is done according to the book.

Cleanup is recommended

If accumulation of unnecessary and obsolete documents is a problem, implementation of ISO 9000 in the design department should start by ordering a large trash container. There is no reason to keep catalogs that are 10 years old. The same with magazines, reports, and standards.

What should be kept?

A 20-year-old textbook is fine in a factory that makes fake antiques, but is of no use any other place. Is it necessary to retain every single scrap of paper from closed-out projects? To help decide what can be thrown away, and to maintain order in the future, the department could develop a policy for retention periods of various types of documents; instructions for which design project documents should be retained after completion of a project; and how the documents should be filed.

Should reference materials be controlled?

Control of reference materials is a gray area. Strictly speaking, the existing designs that will be used as the basis for the new design, and the standards, theories, methods, and research or testing data should be formally approved. Logic dictates that such approval cannot be meaningful if the reference materials are of unknown quality; i.e., they are not organized, indexed, and reviewed. Indeed, there are industries — medical devices and drugs, for example — that fully control their design reference materials and must list them when seeking FDA approval for new designs. The reference material control system in these companies is based on organizing and cataloging material into a library collection; identification of all superseded documents by stamping them with a HISTORY stamp; and a procedure for approval and admitting of reference material to be used in design.

Reference materials considered design input

ISO 9000 auditors do not expect to see the same degree of control in unregulated industries. However, if an auditor suspects that the reference materials are not retrievable and their use is arbitrary, they will investigate and most likely find a noncompliance. The justification will be that these documents are, in fact, a part of the design input, or that they are used to validate the design and, as such, must be approved before use. Standards, old drawings, and specifications are the most vulnerable to a finding.

Preventive measures

The best approach is to avoid alerting auditors that there could be a problem in this area. The way to do it is to clean up the area, arrange the catalogues and files in neat rows, label every binder to identify its content, and remove all documents from desks and drafting boards that are not being used for the current task at hand.

Control is required for standards providing design input

There are, however, reference documents that must be controlled under any circumstances. These are the international, national, state, municipal, and industry specific standards that are used indirectly to define the design input (all mandatory codes belong to this category, for example). These standards should be kept in a dedicated and segregated location; there should be a current list or catalog with the name, revision, and date of issue of each standard; and there must be a system for updating the standards to ensure that they are on the latest revision level.

Compliance with revision control

Standards that have been purchased with a maintenance service (for instance, their publisher sends updated pages when there is a revision), or standards that are reissued annually, automatically comply with the requirements for revision control. For other standards, there should be a procedure explaining how they are updated. Periodical checking with their publisher or a library (every three months, for example) is a common method. Standards that are not mandatory and are rarely used, but are sometimes referenced in contracts, may just have a label affixed to their cover stating CHECK FOR LATEST REVISION BEFORE USE, and a telephone number to call.

COMPUTER PROGRAMS

There is nothing in ISO 9001 Section 4.4 about computer programs. Companies that do not have a consultant or do not go through pre-audit with a registrar are unlikely to be aware that computer programs are even an issue.

40 ISO 9000 QUALITY SYSTEM

Computer programs are not mentioned in ISO 9000

While auditing the design department is difficult because of requirements that are not precisely stated and the many ways design control can be implemented, the audit of control and validation of computer programs used for developing and verification of design is easy and straightforward. This is one of the reasons why auditors never forget to ask about computer programs.

Issues are revision control, master disks, manuals, and validation

The issues are control of versions and revisions, master disks, operating manuals, and validation. In the case of standard software, such as a CAD system or a popular program for structural calculations, auditors normally do not expect in-house validation. But some may still ask how the design department can be absolutely sure that the software returns correct results. If the manuals contain any reference to testing and validation, it is advisable to be able to point it out, but it really should not be an issue. However, if the purchased software is very specialized and developed by a small company, the auditor will pursue evidence of validation. To avoid the risk of a noncompliance, the company policy should be to always ask for validation certification whenever software is purchased; and the policy should be documented in a procedure.

Validation is mandatory for in-house software

While the establishment of evidence for the validation of purchased software is ambiguous, there is no doubt about this requirement for in-house or modified software. Lack of a validation report or a user manual is a noncompliance. In most cases, the validation report does not need to be very elaborate. At a minimum, it should identify the types of tests that were performed, the test cases and expected results, and the actual test results. Complex software for critical applications should be tested in compliance with ISO 9000-3 Part 3: Guidelines for the application of ISO 9001 to the development, supply, and maintenance of software. After all testing is completed, the validation report and user manuals should be reviewed and approved, and the software released for use by an authorized person.

Shortcut for initial testing and validation requirements

When people hear about the software testing and validation requirements three months before the certification audit, they feel faint. Even with just 5 to 10 in-house software programs, this could be a big job. Fortunately, there is a shortcut that has been previously accepted. Instead of validation reports, an authorized person can issue a written certification for software programs that have been used for, let's say, one year prior to implementation of ISO 9000; in other words, the software can be grandfathered. The written certification needs to state that the software performed satisfactorily on previous projects and has proven itself in service. This will exempt the software from the validation requirement.

But the system must still be implemented

But grandfathering existing software does not eliminate the requirement for a procedure and a system for validating new software and future revisions of the grandfathered software. In short, everything else must be in place, but instead of validation reports, the software control files will contain the grandfathering certificates. This system for validating existing programs must be described in a procedure, and thus be officially approved, issued, and implemented.

Revision control also required

In addition to the validation requirements, there are also control requirements. In-house developed software must be identified by a release, version, or revision number that uniquely identifies the master disks, user disks, validation reports and manuals. Software loaded into a computer should also be identifiable from the computer screen. Every revision of software must be again validated and formally released for use.

Control master disks and user manuals

For either purchased or in-house software, master disks should be labeled to identify them as masters and be stored securely and separately from user disks. Auditors often check disk storage cases and investigate further when they find a questionable disk. All computers, peripherals, and software must have user manuals. It is best if the manuals are stored adjacent to the equipment to which they pertain, but if this is too difficult to control, they can be placed in other locations that are designated for this purpose. Auditors may ask anyone working with equipment or computer programs to show where the manuals are kept; if the person does not know, it could be a noncompliance.

DESIGN REVIEWS

Review design
for feasibility
and suitability

Design reviews are often an important element of the design verification program. This function of design reviews will be discussed in the *Design Verification* section further in this chapter. This section is concerned with more general aspects and functions of design reviews. In addition to verifying that the design output meets the technical requirements of the design input, the design reviews must ensure that environmental, safety, reliability, serviceability, manufacturability, and process requirements are also addressed satisfactorily.

Design reviews
are emphasized

In the initial 1987 edition of ISO 9001, the design reviews were mentioned among other methods for design verification. The new, 1994 revision of the standard elevated the importance of design reviews by dedicating to them a separate subsection. As a result of this change, it is likely that auditors will now devote considerably more attention to design reviews. For larger projects, they will expect to find a schedule of design reviews following every major phase of the project, and will ask for the evidence that the reviews are being conducted. Smaller projects can still comply by having only one review, usually when the design is substantially completed.

Not a progress
or coordination
meeting

A design review meeting is not the same thing as a project progress or coordination meeting, where participation is usually limited to the design group itself and the agenda focuses on organizational, scheduling, and cost related matters. The design review should be open to all parties that may have interest in the design. The usual participants are the designers presenting their design and representatives from marketing, sales, production, and quality assurance departments. In cases when specialized expertise is needed, such as regulatory requirements, safety, product liability, or environmental issues, experts in these disciplines may be also involved.

Presence of a customer or his representative often inhibits others from objectively criticizing the design. They should not, therefore, be invited to design review meetings unless it is a contractual requirement. Customers may participate in the review process by reviewing the design output documentation or attending separate meetings.

From the simplest design project...

The number and scope of design reviews depend on the nature and complexity of the design project. The minimum is one review. When conducted at the completion of design, it can be integrated with design verification and its release for production. At the least the quality assurance department and the department that ordered the design should participate in the review. The manner and scope of the design review must be documented in a procedure. The scope may be defined by a list of the kinds of design aspects that need to be considered. The procedure should also instruct how to establish the design review record.

... to the most complex

While one design review is sufficient for small routine projects, larger design projects should have at least two reviews. The first one should be at the beginning of the project and the other one at the end. The first review can evaluate the early conceptual studies and ensure that the design input is appropriate and complete, and should include requirements related to unintended uses, safety, environmental impact, reliability, serviceability, manufacturability, and so forth. The first review is often combined with the design input review (required in Section 4.4.4).

For large and complex design projects, a design review should be scheduled following every major phase of the project.

There should always be a review at the end of a project. The best time is when all elements of the design are completely defined but the final design output docu-

Final design review is mandatory

ments have not yet been completed. A list of issues that could be considered for the final design review is provided in ISO 9004, Section 8.5. The list contains 22 points. Not all of them are relevant for an average design project, but the list is very helpful in understanding what design reviews are about.

Most common is design review meeting

The most common way to conduct a design review is to organize a meeting. Design reviews can also be conducted by distributing preliminary drawings and drafts of specifications to the interested departments and experts for comments. Or, designers can visit the relevant departments one by one to present the design. In fact, any exposure of the design allowing for objective evaluation from other departments, external experts, the customer, or even colleagues from the design group, will qualify as a design review, or at least a partial review. Whatever the manner of the design review, its conclusions must be recorded. The record can be a memorandum, a report, minutes of a meeting, or in any other form.

DESIGN OUTPUT

Document and implement acceptance criteria and review requirements

Section 4.4.6, Design output, contains four requirements, but only two need to be documented and implemented: point b), the acceptance criteria requirement, and point d), the review requirement. Points a) and c) are obvious and do not require any special action to comply.

In point b), engineers are asked to include or reference acceptance criteria in the design output documents. Most companies already do, but may not have written policies that confirm the implementation of this requirement. Preparing for the certification audit, the appropriate policy should be included in the design control procedure and a sample of drawings and specifications should be checked to make sure that the acceptance criteria are consistently being documented.

In many cases the acceptance criteria are determined by the quality assurance department instead of the design

Must be able to distinguish acceptable product

department and are, therefore, documented in inspection procedures instead of drawings and specifications. There is no problem with doing it this way. Inspection procedures can also be considered design output documents. The bottom line is that inspectors at each inspection point must have clear instructions for how to distinguish an acceptable product from an unacceptable one.

Specify tolerances on dimensions

The most frequent noncompliance with this requirement is the lack of specified tolerances on dimensions or other parameters. If a drawing shows that a certain dimension should be two inches, and there is no general note, policy, or procedure explaining what the acceptable deviation is, theoretically all products should be rejected — nothing measures exactly two inches except for the national standard. Although a noncompliance may seem unreasonable because tolerances are obvious, this is an international standard and we cannot be sure that they will be just as obvious when the drawings are sent to another country.

Review, approve, and release

Point d) of Section 4.4.6 requires that all design output documents must be reviewed before release. The review methods are discussed in the design review section of this chapter. The implementation of the review requirement is very simple. Every drawing, specification, and manufacturing instruction must be signed and dated by an authorized person to identify it as being approved and released. A procedure should assign the responsibility and authority for the review and approval of the design output documents, and should instruct how to distinguish between draft or preliminary documents and final documents that are approved for production.

DESIGN VERIFICATION AND VALIDATION

Method of verification depends on complexity of design

Although the systems for verifying a space shuttle design and a toothbrush design will be very different, in both cases auditors will refer to the same text in ISO 9001 Section 4.4.7 and 4.4.8. This is the most striking example of the degree to which the standard must be interpreted in the context to which it is applied. Trying to describe a generic system for design verification and validation is not possible. Every company must decide how to comply with these requirements for its own situation.

Verify that the design output satisfies design input

It is important to understand that the objective of design verification is not just the mechanical checking of drawings and specifications. The objective is to verify that the design output meets the design input requirements. The analogy from the manufacturing environment is the inspection of the final completed product. To be sure, checking of drawings is also required. Errors in drawings can cause quality problems in production. But a perfectly drafted drawing does not necessarily represent a good design and, vice versa, inadequate drawings can represent very good designs. There is no relation between the quality of design and the quality of drawings that represent it.

From the simplest design project...

The simplest design verification system suitable for a small company with fairly routine design projects could comprise the following elements:

- a procedure describing the design verification scope and methods, and providing instructions how to establish the verification records;

- a person or a body responsible for conducting design verifications and authorized to release the design;

- records evidencing that designs are being verified before they are released for production.

The responsibility for design verification could be assigned to the head of the design department and/or representatives from other departments, such as marketing, sales, production, and quality assurance. The procedure should clearly state that the objective of the verification is to establish that the design output meets the design input requirements, and should obligate the reviewer to systematically analyze the design against all design input elements and additional criteria that might apply, including safety, serviceability, environmental impact, regulatory requirements, etc. The conclusions of the design verification can be recorded in a memorandum, minutes of a meeting, or in any other suitable form.

... to the most complex

For larger and more complex design projects, design verification programs should not be limited to only one final verification. Analogous to in-process inspections of products, there should also be in-process design verifications. The in-process verifications should be scheduled following every major design phase and at interfaces where data is transferred from one design group to another.

At the end of the preliminary or conceptual design phase, for example, the verification is usually conducted by way of a design review meeting where the marketing, sales, production, and quality assurance departments are given the opportunity to check whether their requirements are being satisfactorily implemented. Minutes of the design review meetings or a memorandum with its conclusions is an acceptable record evidencing that the design verification has been conducted at this stage.

Checking data transmitted between various design groups or passing between design phases is another common form of in-process verification. For example, Isabel's vibration analysis will be reviewed by Thomas, and a sample of the new insulating material proposed by Alex will be sent to a lab for testing before it is used in the design.

Should be capable of responding to design changes

The design verification plan should be capable of responding to any design input changes and other unforeseen changes introduced during the design project. Returning to the insulating material example above, it would have been impossible to predict at the beginning of the project that Alex would find a new insulating material that was only half the thickness of the material used in previous designs of similar products. The new material could significantly reduce the size of the whole product — a great advantage — but, before the design is directed to exploit this new possibility, the insulating material must be tested to verify that it performs as claimed and is suitable in other respects. Now the verification plan must be updated to add the lab testing, and some design activities must be put on hold awaiting the results.

Planning and documentation often overlooked

Such verification activities are customary and are not new to designers. The ISO 9001 requirement that these in-process verification activities also be planned and documented is seldom complied with, however. The design verification plan is equivalent to the activity assignment plan discussed earlier. In fact, the design project planning and scheduling chart, presented in the *Design Planning* section of this chapter, contains a column for in-process verification activities. Not all design phases and activities must be followed by a review. The scope of the verification plan will not be questioned by auditors as long as it is coherent and sufficient to achieve its objectives.

Establish records

The record of in-process verifications can be established by a reviewer's sign-off, an entry in a design project log, a memorandum, minutes of a meeting, a report, or a certificate. The reviewer, the reviewing body, or the certifying authority should be identified on the record. The in-process review records should be organized and indexed so that they can be presented at the final design review meeting. The records will provide evidence that design complies with design input requirements.

Final verification is mandatory

While the in-process verifications are optional and will only be expected for more complex design projects, the final verification and release of the design is mandatory, regardless how small and simple the design. The requirements for design verification are analogous to those pertaining to inspection and testing of products. The products are compared to their technical documentation, while in design, the design output is compared with the design input.

For more complex projects, the final verification should start with checking that all specified in-process verifications have been completed successfully and that, indeed, the design is completed. The design is then checked against each design input requirement. The demonstration and evidence that the design meets those requirements can be a simple comparison of the design output with the design input, comparison of the design with a similar proven design, or qualification tests and demonstrations.

A simple comparison between what was required and the actual features of the design is appropriate when the input requirements are stated as specific data that can be directly identified on drawings, specifications, or other design output documents; such as dimensions, weight, materials, colors, etc. When the input contains performance data of functional requirements, for example, strength, speed, efficiency, or capability to do a specific thing, the design should also be supported by calculations or comparisons with similar proven designs. The ultimate verification is building and testing a model or a prototype and, if this is the case, the whole verification process will center around the obtained test results.

Final verification can be a design review meeting

The most common format of the final design verification is a design review meeting. At the meeting, the designers present the design to other interested parties and demonstrate that it meets the design input requirements. The participants of the meeting can be given the authority to formally accept and approve the design. Minutes of the design review meeting or a memorandum documenting its conclusions should be retained as the record evidencing that the final design verification was carried out.

To be independently verified or not to be...

Another aspect of design verification is independence of the reviewer from those responsible for the design or any of its elements. While ISO 9000 unquestionably allows self-inspection of products, it is not entirely clear that the same is true for design verification. In the 1987 edition of the standard it was explicitly stated that design reviews (and audits) shall be carried out by personnel independent from those having direct responsibility for the design. The fact that this statement somehow disappeared from the 1994 version of the standard does not change the logic behind the distinction between verification of a product and verification of design.

Product drawings and specifications usually define a product in very specific and precise terms, and an inspection to verify that the product complies with those documents is often just a matter of a simple measurement. On the other hand, design input requirements are often not so precisely stated and evaluating whether the design satisfies the requirements generally involves a judgment. From this point of view, it is logical that the person making the design judgment should not be appointed to make an unbiased judgment to verify it.

While this is, I believe, the only correct interpretation of the standard, auditors normally do not object to self-verification unless there are no records or some other evidence that the verification was carried out at all. A statement such as "He always checks his calculations again before turning them in." is not acceptable. A pragmatic approach is to allow for self-verification (but as a distinct and recorded activity) in cases where the verification is a simple checking or comparison against precisely stated requirements. In other cases, when interpretation and judgment are involved, an independent person should be assigned to carry out the review.

Review and approve design output documents

The last issue in this section is the review of the design output documents for completeness and correctness. As discussed previously in the *Design Output* section of this chapter, the review and verification of the design output drawings and specifications cannot substitute for a true design verification. Once the design has been reviewed and verified, the purpose of reviewing the design output documents is to avoid production problems due to mistakes in drawings and specifications. The scope of the document review should include coordination of drawings of different views and cross-sections, or different installations (for example: structural, electrical, hydraulic, etc.) to avoid discrepancies and conflicts; checking tolerances, process notes, surface finish instructions, etc.; and a review of material lists. The types of design output documents that must be verified and the general scope of the review should be documented in a procedure or work instructions. A sign-off on the approved document is sufficient evidence and record of the review.

DESIGN CHANGES

Fully develop and document design change system

Systems for controlling design changes already exist in most companies, although to pass ISO 9000 they may need to be further developed and documented in procedures. ISO 9001 Section 4.4.9, Design changes, is very short — only 18 words. But four of those words, namely: *identified, documented, reviewed,* and *approved* tell us precisely what the minimum acceptable scope is for this system.

"Design Change Request" form

Identification of desired or required design changes may come from marketing, sales, production, servicing, quality assurance, or the design department itself. They can also come from external sources such as customers, regulatory agencies or product liability cases. A procedure should list these sources and instruct how they should document their requests and communicate them to the design department. A common way is to use a form — it could be called "Design Change Request" — on which the requesting party can describe the change and state the reasons for the request. Companies that do not have many design changes and do not want to introduce yet another form can just state in a procedure what should be included in a written request for a design change, while leaving the format of the document open.

Review and approve design change

The next step is review and approval of the requests. A procedure should identify who is responsible for handling the requests and should explain the process. If a form is used, there could be a section in the form reserved for recording the review, including: the accept/reject decision, reasons for rejection, instructions for further routing or processing of the request, and signature of the reviewer. When the format is not prescribed, the same information can be recorded in a letter or a memo. The reviewer should inform the requesting party of the decision.

Translate change into design input

At this point the design change request can be translated into a set of specific design input requirements and fed into the regular design control system. In some cases the design change may require organization of a project similar in scope to the original design project but, normally, it will be a condensed version. Nonetheless, there should always be an assignment of a person or a team to carry out the design change, some form of verification, and approval and release of the changed design. To document these activities, a procedure can either describe a separate system for controlling the design change process, or simply state that all relevant rules for controlling original design projects will be applied.

DESIGN OUTPUT DOCUMENT CONTROL

Centralized vs distributed document control

There are two types of document control systems. One is a centralized system operated by a special department or unit that controls the masters and distribution of copies for all documents issued in the company, including the design output documents. The other is a distributed system where each department controls its own documents, and thus the design output documents are controlled by the design department itself.

Centralized systems are suitable for large companies or manufacturers of regulated products, such as medical devices, drugs, nuclear, etc. These systems offer a higher degree of control, but are inefficient and expensive to maintain. Most medium-sized and smaller companies operate the distributed system of document control. ISO 9000 does not require any specific organization and, if a distributed system works well, there is no reason to change it.

To comply with ISO 9001 Section 4.5, Document and data control, a control system for design output documents should regulate the following activities: review,

Document control requirements

approval, and release of documents; cataloging, index-ing, filing, and retrieval of masters; document copying and distribution; review, approval, and release of docu-ment changes; distribution of new revisions and removal of obsolete documents; marking and storage of obsolete "history" masters.

The design department does not have to be responsible for all these functions. In this book I make the assump-tion that distribution of new and revised documents and removal of obsolete documents is the responsibility of the production planning department, and this function will not be discussed here. The requirements for review, approval, and release of documents are discussed in pre-ceding sections and are also omitted from this section. The remaining topics are storage of the current and superseded masters and a system for their control and retrieval.

Storage, control, and retrieval are critical

Any system that does not provide for dedicated and seg-regated locations for storage of master drawings, spec-ifications, and originals of other product-related docu-ments is bound to fail the certification audit. Mixing originals with copies, storing documents in piles on top of desks or cabinets, or keeping them in private offices and work areas is unacceptable. The storage locations must be identified and authorized. Auditors usually do not like to see the storage areas for master documents being used for other purposes, such as storage of office supplies, old files, reference materials. or catalogs. As long as there is no direct intermingling, however, this is not a noncompliance.

A well-defined area will suffice

A separate and secured room dedicated exclusively for storage of master documents is the best solution. If this is not practical or possible, a well-defined area in the general office will suffice. In very small companies, even a single cabinet or rack designated for storage of masters is acceptable as long as it is separated and identified. The trouble starts when one drawer of the cabinet contains masters, the next one some "personal" stuff, the third some more masters, and the fourth a few unfinished drawings, a poster, and drafting paper. Every drawer, rack, shelf, or cabinet containing the master documents needs to be labeled, identifying its contents.

Catalog and index documents

Once the original documents are properly stored, they must be cataloged and indexed to allow for revision level control and easy retrieval. The system can operate by way of a computer database, catalog cards, registers, lists, and so forth. All active documents must be included in the system and, as a minimum, be identified by their title and/or number, and current revision level.

Segregate and clearly identify obsolete documents

The requirements for segregation of superseded documents from the active documents is a gray area. Many companies store all revisions of a document in the same file. Auditors generally question this type of arrangement. Even though every document has its revision number indicated on it and there is a list specifying current revision levels of documents, an obsolete version can be confused with the current version when all are in the same file. A practical way to remove any doubt is to stamp the superseded documents with a large red HISTORY or OBSOLETE stamp. If regulated products are involved, it is expected that the obsolete masters are stored in a separate location.

Control master documents

Access to the master documents and their removal for revising and copying should be controlled. A simple system can comprise restriction of access to the master document storage area; use of checkout cards for removing documents; and recording of all copying. In small companies these arrangements can operate as self-service, and if only a very small group of people is involved, some of the control elements may be left out. For instance, document checkout cards would not be reasonable if there are only three people that have access to the master documents.

No matter how small and simple the system is, controlling the document copying activities is useful for many reasons. A copying log not only provides a record of the correct documents being copied, but also contributes to the control of copying costs and protects the company's proprietary information from unauthorized distribution.

CONTROL OF OTHER DOCUMENTS

Parts lists, bills of materials, traceability logs, etc., must also be controlled

Other kinds of documents that the design department may need to control are product configuration logs and files, bills of materials, parts lists, specification sheets for purchased products, manufacturing instructions, logs with assignment of serial numbers and configuration traceability, samples, workmanship standards, and any other type of document generated by the department.

Some of the documents listed above will not be issued by the design department, especially in larger companies. Indeed, the organization presented in this book has a production planning department that is responsible for these kind of things. The next chapter is dedicated to this department.

Determine type of documents and type of control

When preparing for the certification audit, the design department should draft a list of all the documents that it produces and ask the following questions:

- Do we approve and formally release these documents?
- How is their approval and release recorded?
- Are these documents cataloged in a list, a log, or a computer database?
- Do we have a designated storage location for these documents?
- How can anyone find out what is their current revision level?
- How do we protect masters and control copying?

Not all of the above questions will be answered in the affirmative for all documents. Project correspondence, for example, does not need to be approved, does not have revision numbers, and does not need to be copied for distribution; but it may be required to be logged and, certainly, should have a designated filing place, such as a project book, for example.

The auditor may ask...

While auditing the design department, auditors may pick up a random file, or even a sheet of paper, and ask: "What is it?.., Which project does it belong to?.., Why is it here?.., Is this its regular storage location?.., May I see other documents of this type?.., What is the distribution of these documents?.." And so forth. The answers are usually satisfactory when an important document, such as a drawing, is involved. But unless the same care and attention is taken, secondary documents and lists or logs for management of other documents often fail somewhere along the line of such questioning.

6 PRODUCTION PLANNING

No corresponding section in ISO 9000

ISO 9000 does not have a section that directly corresponds to a production planning and scheduling department. Also, production planning and scheduling functions are not organized into independent departments in many companies. These functions are often shared by sales, production, and design departments. Because of the lack of visibility in both the ISO 9000 standards and in a company's organization, these functions can be easily overlooked. For these reasons many companies do not adequately prepare production planning and scheduling for the ISO 9000 certification audit.

Plan, schedule, and document

While I am not recommending that an independent department is necessary for the production planning and scheduling functions, I decided to include such a department in this book to ensure that preparation of these functions for the certification audit will not be overlooked. The responsibilities of this production planning and scheduling department can be divided into three categories:

- to plan production by defining the individual production operations and processes, and their sequence;
- to schedule production; and,
- to document the production plan and schedule in the form of a work order, and issue the work order to the production department.

Implement in relevant departments

Each category will be discussed under a separate heading. In companies that do not have a single department responsible for all three functions, the ISO 9000 requirements discussed in this chapter must be implemented in the departments where they apply.

PLANNING OPERATIONS AND PROCESSES

"How do production personnel know what operations and processes are required to manufacture a product?"

ISO 9000 section 4.9, Process control, states: "The supplier shall identify and plan the production . . . processes." To assess compliance with this statement in the standard, auditors often ask directly, "How do you plan your production processes and how is the plan documented?" When confronted with this question people often do not know what to answer. They instinctively think that the auditor is asking for a document entitled Production Process Plan. Most likely such a document does not exist in their company. The question would be better understood if auditors asked, "How do production personnel know what operations and processes, and their sequence, are required to manufacture a product?"

By physical layout

A production plan can be expressed in many forms and does not even need to be documented. In its simplest form, a production plan can be implied in the physical arrangement of the production area. For example, process machines and individual work stations could be positioned in the same sequence as the planned production operations, forcing the production flow into a predetermined path. To eliminate any doubt, the work stations could be numbered sequentially. In my opinion, in companies where production is constant and it is obvious that there are no alternative ways to process a product, or sequence the processing, such implied expression of the production plan should be sufficient to comply with ISO 9000. There are, however, auditors that can only be satisfied with a piece of paper. To avoid any problems, even in such simple and obvious situations, it is preferable to have something written down. The production plan listing the production operations could be a short procedure or a note on a drawing.

In industries today, companies often redesign their products, add new products and configurations, and frequently process custom orders. In this environment, a permanent arrangement of work flow is not practical. When production changes are frequent, the best way to

By documenting operations and processes of the production cycle

document a production plan is by listing the operations and processes on a work order, traveler, flow tag or other such document that accompanies products, or batches of products, through their production cycle. In this book I refer to a work order as the generic name for this document. A work order can be an invaluable tool for satisfying many requirements of ISO 9000. Work orders are discussed in detail in the last section of this chapter.

And by referencing drawings and specifications

The production plan, whether documented in a work order or another type of document, should be a sequential listing of all operations and processes required to manufacture a product or a subassembly. The first operation could be to pull and stage the raw materials and parts, with reference to a specific bill of materials or drawing. The second operation could be material treatment, such as cleaning or painting. Each subsequent operation and process would be listed until the product is completed. Applicable drawings, specifications, work procedures or workmanship standards should be referenced in the plan at every step as required.

By a flow diagram

When products are assembled from subassemblies that are manufactured on different production lines, the plan can be a flow diagram that identifies the operations for each subassembly, and when and how they are assembled into the finished product. When work orders are used, each subassembly and the assembly operations could be guided by a separate work order.

A quality plan can be included in production plan

The production plan is often combined with the quality plan. This can be accomplished by inserting the required inspection or testing operations between the production processes. When applicable, specific inspection and testing procedures and acceptance criteria should be referenced for every quality operation. More detailed discussion of the quality plans will follow in Chapter 11, Quality Control.

Cases where auditors identify a noncompliance for the complete lack of a production plan are rare. It is more often the environment and the way in which produc-

Control: review and approve reference documents

tion plans are generated that is the reason for concern. Production plans are the result of certain technological know-how and experience. Establishing a production plan requires referencing and analyzing drawings, specifications, and standards. In this context, auditors will be interested in the controls employed to ensure that all these reference documents are approved and are on the current revision level.

Duplicate vs master files

Especially vulnerable are those production planning departments that like to store copies of drawings and specifications in their own files. If this is the case, auditors will be eager to find out how the parallel or duplicate files are controlled and maintained. In other words, what is done to ensure that only current revisions of drawings and specifications are in the files? While the master files controlled by the design department do not usually cause serious problems, duplicate files are very often areas of noncompliance. Whenever practical and possible, drawings and specifications should be issued on an as-needed basis and then discarded after use.

Document control: review and approve production plan

The production plans, whether established as separate documents or contained in work orders, are in themselves controlled documents. Accordingly, they must be reviewed and approved before issue and, if applicable, be identified with a revision level. In the case of work orders, review and approval is often overlooked, particularly when they are computer generated (refer to the last section of this chapter).

PRODUCTION SCHEDULING

Scheduling is an implied requirement

Production scheduling, while not directly mandated anywhere in the ISO 9000 standards, is strongly implied in Section 4.3, Contract review. Therein the supplier is obliged to verify the capacity to meet contract or accepted order requirements. Delivery date is almost always a contractual requirement and, obviously, without production scheduling there is no way to tell if sufficient capacity will be available to process an order.

Schedule changes need to be communicated

The format, time interval used, degree of detail, and updating frequency will be very different from one industry to another. In most cases a simple bar schedule, or even a list, showing when accepted orders will be fed into individual production lines, is sufficient. But at the other extreme, there are also industries that need to constantly maintain integrated real-time computer models of all their production operations.

As a rule, auditors will not try to assess the adequacy of the scheduling system unless it is an obvious farce; the benefit of doubt is given to the auditee. Auditors would rather concentrate on investigating how information required to update the schedule is obtained, if the schedule is maintained regularly, and how information regarding production capacity is communicated to sales.

None of this must necessarily be described in procedures. Auditors are generally satisfied if there is evidence that the required information is obtained from identified sources and current documents; that updating is sufficiently frequent to keep pace with the average rate of incoming orders; and that there is a two-way channel for communicating with the sales department.

Audit scheduling function

A common technique used by auditors is to first inquire about any recent production line or major processing machine breakdown and the time it took to bring it back. They then analyze if this event was reflected in production scheduling. If orders accepted after the breakdown were started and/or delivered late because of the delay of orders that were impacted by the breakdown, it is clear that either the schedule was not updated or the schedule change was not communicated to sales. Generally, auditors will be looking carefully for a pattern of late deliveries and will ask for reasons in individual cases. Unsatisfactory schedule performance may open a can of worms. Typically, not only would production scheduling be questioned, but also the systems for contract review, internal auditing, and corrective action.

Individual schedules for larger projects

Larger production projects should have individual schedules. Larger projects are usually orders for complex custom or customized products. The schedule can either be a CPM or a bar schedule. It should be sufficiently detailed to allow for coordinating in-house manufacturing with subcontracting as well as completion of major subassemblies within the final assembling deadlines. It should contain allowance for in-process and final inspections and testing. In many companies, even those that manufacture standard products, individual order scheduling is included in work orders containing the planned start and completion dates for all subassemblies, products, or batches. Auditors will not expect single order scheduling unless it is a project with complex purchasing, subcontracting, and other interfacing, for example, a large machine, a ship, a building, etc.

WORK ORDERS

The document that initiates manufacturing

There are many names for the document that initiates manufacture of a product, or a batch or series of products (also parts and subassemblies): work order, traveler, shop ticket, flow tag, routing card, to name a few. The name depends on the physical appearance of the document, as well as the jargon used in a given industry or company. I refer to a *work order* here because it seems to be the most widely used term.

More than a production plan

In the preceding section the work order was presented as an excellent instrument for documenting a production plan. The work order can also be an invaluable tool for satisfying many other requirements of ISO 9000. It can be used to identify the product; define and document the quality plan; become an inspection record; serve as a configuration and traceability record; and track the use of time and resources.

Is the work order suitable for smaller companies?

Although implementation of ISO 9000 may be more difficult when work orders are not used, smaller companies that do not use work orders should not try to introduce them solely for the purpose of ISO 9000 certification. Introduction of work orders is a major change in the way a company functions, and it may significantly delay the certification schedule. There is nothing in ISO 9000 about work orders being mandatory.

Expand the functionality of work order

In companies where work orders are already in use, but are not being used for all the functions that could benefit the implementation of ISO 9000, it will usually pay to modify the work order system. Adding a function to the work order, such as quality plan requirements or inspection status identification, is often simpler than implementing other solutions.

Manage the work order

Establishing and managing work orders can range from a simple form that is filled out manually, to an integrated computer system with automated bar code data input. The most typical system used in mid-sized and smaller companies today is computer-generated forms, cards, or tickets that are processed manually at various operations during the production cycle. In companies that often manufacture custom or customized products, the work orders are accompanied by a packet of documents containing drawings, specifications, process procedures, and other documents instructing how to manufacture and inspect the products. Conversely, where the production is constant, documents of this kind may be permanently placed at relevant work stations, which eliminates the need to enclose them with the work order.

Determine the work order functions

Although the primary function of the work order is to initiate and monitor production, the potential functionality, listed and described below, is much broader in scope. This additional functionality can help satisfy various quality requirements of the ISO 9000 standards. All potential functions may not be relevant for some companies, such as traceability, and some functions may already be implemented in other ways. In companies where the work order system is fully automated and people do not write anything on work orders, adding any new functions may not be practical. Thus, each company must judge for itself which functions from the following list to adopt in their work orders. As in other parts of this book, the word *product* is used here to mean

64   ISO 9000 QUALITY SYSTEM

part, subassembly, product, or batches of products.

List operations and processes

Production plan: The production plan, referenced in ISO 9000 Section 4.9, can be documented in a work order and is a listing of all operations and processes required to manufacture a product or a subassembly. For every operation or process where the use of drawings, specifications, work procedures or workmanship standards are required, the applicable document should be referenced, or be attached to the work order.

List quality control operations

Quality plan: Quality plans are specifically required in ISO 9000 Section 4.2.3 and are mentioned in a couple of other sections. The quality plan can be documented in a work order, to include inspection and testing operations. Each quality operation, such as in-process inspection, is inserted after the applicable production operation or process, the result of which must be verified. In this case, the last operation on the work order would be the final inspection or test operation. If the scope, method, or acceptance criteria for a given inspection is not obvious, a reference to a relevant drawing or inspection procedure should be included.

Use to identify product

Product identification: ISO 9000 Section 4.8 requires that products be identified during all stages of production. If the work order accompanies the product very closely — as a tag or a ticket does, for example — and the name, type, style, catalog number, etc., are stated on the work order, then the work order can be considered to also identify the product, and thereby compliance with Section 4.8 is achieved. But, again, the condition is that the work order is attached to the product, or it is otherwise evident at all times which work order pertains to which specific product or batch.

Record traceability

Traceability: If traceability is required, ISO 9000 Section 4.8, the serial number is identified on the work order before it is possible to label the product itself. For every operation and process that must be traceable, operators can enter on the work order the identifications of their work station, process machine used, serial or batch numbers of parts and raw materials, and any other records that may be required to assure traceability. After the product is completed, the work order constitutes the record of traceability.

Use for record of inspection

Inspection record: A sign-off or inspection stamp in the field adjacent to where an inspection operation is called out constitutes a valid record of the inspection. If the inspection results need to be recorded and/or the inspection equipment needs to be identified, this can also be recorded on the work order, or on a separate report that is then referenced to assure traceability. This function in the work order will fully comply with ISO 9000 section 4.10.5, Inspection and Test Records.

Use to identify inspection status

Inspection and test status: ISO 9000 Section 4.12 requires that inspection and test status of product be identified throughout production. If the work order accompanies the product, contains the quality plan (i.e. calls out inspections), and has the provision for the inspection sign-offs, the inspection status is self-evident. Sign-off indicates a passed inspection and an empty space means on hold, awaiting inspection. A failed inspection can be identified by other means, such as a red tag or label and segregation.

Document the work order functions

If the work order is used for any of these functions, there should be a procedure explaining how the function is implemented in this way. It is best to have one dedicated procedure that deals with all aspects of the work order, but the same can be achieved by explaining its use in separate specialized procedures dealing with identification, traceability, inspections, and so forth. When there is a dedicated work order procedure, it is sufficient to reference it in the other specialized procedures.

At the time when the work order is established, it is a document. It contains important instructions on how to manufacture and inspect a product. But after completion of the product, it becomes a record. It contains traceability data and inspection sign-offs. Thus the work order must comply with both ISO 9000 Section 4.5, Doc-

**A document
and a record**

ument and data control, and ISO 9000 Section 4.16, Control of quality records. As a controlled document, the work order should be reviewed and approved before issue. In the case of constant and standard production, where the production and quality plans do not change and work orders are printed from a computer where only quantities, job numbers, and completion dates are changed, individual printouts do not need to be approved separately. It is sufficient that there is an approved master on file.

Otherwise, every work order must be signed off to evidence approval before issue. A procedure should name the personnel authorized to carry out the review and approval. Other requirements of ISO 9000 Section 4.5, such as revision status, master list, document placement and removal, are not applicable for the work order.

**Evidence of
quality plan
review and
approval**

If a work order prescribes inspection and testing operations, i.e., documents a quality plan, the production planning and scheduling department can be questioned about the quality plan. Auditors will expect that the quality assurance department is involved in this matter. To demonstrate that this is indeed the case, quality assurance should prepare the quality plan and approve the work order with respect to quality requirements or, at a minimum, issue a written policy explaining the extent of required inspections and/or testing.

 # PURCHASING DEPARTMENT

Evaluate subcontractors and provide purchasing data

ISO 9000 Section 4.6.2, Evaluation of subcontractors, and Section 4.6.3, Purchasing data, contain the two principal requirements that must be implemented in the purchasing department. The first one calls for evaluating, qualifying, and monitoring subcontractors, and the other pertains to the control and verification of purchasing data. Traditional quality systems usually do not control the purchasing activities to the degree required by ISO 9000. Preparing for certification, most companies will need to profoundly improve their purchasing control systems, and many will be starting from the beginning.

Customers permitted to verify purchased product

In addition to the two principal requirements of Sections 4.6.2 and 4.6.3, there is also Section 4.6.4, Verification of purchased products. This section deals with product verification at the subcontractor's premises. The section is not relevant for many companies, and even when it is, there are no requirements that must be implemented. A policy statement in the quality manual confirming that, when specified in the contract, customers shall be afforded the right to verify products at the subcontractor's premises, will be sufficient to comply with this section.

Suppliers of standard product vs custom/critical product

For most companies it is unreasonable and inefficient to use the same system for evaluation and selection of all subcontractors without regard for the nature of the purchased products. Purchasing of standard, noncritical materials and components does not need to follow the same strict criteria that are applicable when custom and/or critical products are involved. To distinguish between the two groups of products, the vendors can be divided into two categories: suppliers and subcontractors.

Suppliers and subcontractors

In this book, *suppliers* are defined as those vendors that supply noncritical standard catalog products, while *subcontractors* are defined as vendors supplying products that are either modified to or manufactured from the company's drawings and specifications, or are intended for a critical application. This distinction may not be applicable in some companies, while others may want to increase the number of different categories of vendors. I have chosen these two groups, as this seems to represent the most common situation and can serve as an example of how a system requiring different degrees of control for different cases can be implemented not only for purchasing, but for almost any other quality system element.

Always includes production-related product

An often asked question is: What categories of purchased products can be completely excluded from the control of the quality system in purchasing and receiving inspection? It is an important question because it really asks about the scope of application of the ISO 9000 standard. Unfortunately, there is no clear answer for all cases. Without any doubt, all materials, components, and subassemblies intended for incorporation into the final product offering, including spare parts, manuals, and packaging, must be subjected to all requirements of the standard. Also, without any doubt, all office, janitorial, safety, and other supplies and furniture that have no relation to the final product quality can be excluded from the requirements of the standard.

What about production-related equipment?

The gray area between these two categories are products such as production machines and equipment, tooling, handling, and transportation equipment, testing and measuring equipment, and other such items that process, verify, or at least come into contact with the product. Many auditors accept that machines and equipment need not be subjected to purchasing controls and receiving inspection, while other auditors (who I believe are in the minority) hold the opposite view: anything that can potentially impact quality of products must be controlled.

Compromise to include special tooling and verification equipment

The ISO 9000 standard seems to support the narrow interpretation. Section 3, Definitions, states that whenever the word product is used, the requirements apply to "intended product" only. However, I have personally witnessed many noncompliances and failed audits because of these differences in interpretation. To avoid disputes and problems, I would advise a compromise solution: include special tooling designed for a specific product (molds, for example) and the test and measuring equipment intended for verification of the product; and exclude all other machines and equipment.

Include suppliers of delivery services

Suppliers of services for delivery, installation, and servicing must also be included in the vendor evaluation and monitoring system. A very common noncompliance is lack of pre-evaluation and monitoring of the shippers contracted to deliver products to customers. In practice this applies to air freight and trucking companies. I have yet to see a noncompliance given for lack of evaluation and monitoring of the U.S. postal service.

SUPPLIERS OF NONCRITICAL STANDARD PRODUCTS

Suppliers must be evaluated and documented

When noncritical standard products are involved and there is no history of serious quality problems, evaluation, qualification, and monitoring of suppliers does not need to be very elaborate. A minimal system that only just satisfies the requirements of ISO 9000 is sufficient in most cases. However, the implementation of even the most basic requirements in this area may seem somewhat overwhelming and unreasonable to many companies. People get annoyed when they are told they have to evaluate and monitor their paint suppliers. But, reasonable or not, there is no way out. ISO 9000 clearly states that all vendors of materials and components intended for incorporation into the final product must be evaluated. There is no provision for any exceptions.

The most basic system that satisfies the requirements ISO 9000 Section 4.6.2 must comprise:

- A procedure explaining how new suppliers are evaluated and approved, and what controls are exercised over the suppliers;

- A supplier quality record file established for each supplier, containing the initial evaluation record and records evidencing the exercised controls; and,

- An approved supplier list distributed to all personnel involved in issuing requisitions and purchase orders.

Provide evidence of evaluation

The evaluation of suppliers of noncritical standard products does not need to be very extensive, but there must be something in the suppliers quality record files to evidence that the evaluation was undertaken. It can be, for example, a supplier data card containing information related to the supplier's capacity and quality capability. The information may include description of the facilities, number of employees, number of years in business, type of the implemented quality system and its certification status, scope of the final inspection, and a couple of references. This information can be obtained by a telephone interview. If any of the references were contacted, a quick handwritten note can be enclosed as a record. Brochures and catalogs can be also included in the supplier's file unless they are too bulky, in which case a note stating where they are located can be included instead.

Provide record of approval

A formal record of supplier approval could be an approval status sheet with approvals, notices, and disqualifications recorded by an authorized person. The approval status sheet can be permanently attached to the inside cover of the supplier quality record file, so that the supplier's status can be quickly confirmed without the need to browse through the whole file.

The quality assurance, production, or design departments do not need to be involved in the evaluation and approval of suppliers. To streamline the process, it can be entirely controlled by the purchasing department.

Auditors usually do not have very high expectations when standard catalog products are involved. They will be satisfied as long as there is a written procedure and every supplier has a quality record file. The scope and content of the evaluation are normally not questioned, unless an empty file is found.

Established suppliers can be grandfathered

There is a special case when an evaluation record can be substituted by a certificate grandfathering the supplier. It applies to companies that have been operating their quality system only for a short period of time before the certification audit. Existing suppliers that have performed satisfactorily for at least six months prior to implementation of ISO 9000 can be exempted from the requirement for the initial evaluation. The quality record files still need to be established but, instead of the evidence of evaluation, they will contain a certificate, signed by purchasing and quality assurance, stating that the supplier is being approved based on performance history. There will be also, as for all other suppliers, the approval status sheet with appropriate approval authorization. This system for grandfathering existing suppliers must be documented in a procedure, and thus be officially sanctioned.

Appropriate supplier corrective actions and follow-up should satisfy control

The second requirement of Section 4.6.2, exercising control over suppliers, can be satisfied by monitoring the supplier's quality performance and requesting corrective actions when performance is not satisfactory. Some auditors challenge this kind of control, arguing that this is merely collecting quality performance data and reacting only after the damage is done; whereas real control should be aimed at prevention. This argument, however, should not hold. It is true for the performance monitoring part, however, the corrective actions do have the preventive element, as they force the supplier to examine the root causes of the problems and to prevent the same kind of problem from happening again. Auditees must remember this argument and defend it vigorously because any other type of supplier control would require visiting and auditing the supplier. This would impose an unacceptable delay and expense on both parties. However, this defense will not work if it is limited only to verbal arguments. The contents of the supplier quality record files must demonstrate that corrective actions are indeed being requested and followed up.

Implement control system and document procedure

In practice, this system can be implemented by requiring that whenever there is a nonconformity or late delivery, a nonconformity report is prepared and a copy of it is filed in the supplier's quality record file. The supplier is always contacted and informed of the identified nonconformity. If it is sufficiently serious or recurring, purchasing or quality assurance requests the supplier to propose and implement a corrective action and report back on its effectiveness. Copies of all resulting correspondence are kept in the supplier's quality record file. Suppliers who repeatedly fail to deliver satisfactory products and/or do not deliver on time despite earlier complaints and requests for corrective actions are disqualified and removed from the approved supplier list. The disqualification is recorded on the approval status sheet. This or a similar system must be documented in a procedure and the supplier quality records must be maintained regularly to provide the evidence of compliance.

List of approved suppliers should be accessible

The approval status of suppliers must be available to the personnel preparing and/or reviewing purchase orders and, depending on the purchasing system, those who issue requisitions for purchasing. In a very small company where only a few persons are involved with purchasing, the supplier's files may be consulted directly to verify their approval status. In larger companies there should be a list of approved suppliers, established on the basis of their approval status, as recorded in the suppliers' quality record files. In this case, a procedure should instruct who is responsible for generating the list, how often it ought to be updated, and what is its distribution. The list is considered a controlled document and thus must be approved before issue and be identified with a revision level or a date. Auditors will check if the list is in agreement with the supplier quality record files.

SUBCONTRACTORS FOR CRITICAL AND CUSTOM PRODUCTS

Custom or critical products are a higher risk

While evaluation of suppliers for standard catalog products is mostly an exercise in complying with ISO 9000, the need for evaluation of suppliers for critical and custom products is very real. Most companies evaluate their subcontractors regardless of ISO 9000. This process need only be formalized to comply with the standard. The fundamental difference lies in a custom product being, at least in part, defined by the buyer (your company). It does not exist at the time of purchase. In consequence, the uncertainty and risk involved are much greater. The risk is further increased by the comparatively long lead time required for designing and manufacturing a custom product. If the subcontractor fails, the product cannot be immediately purchased somewhere else, and the production schedule can be seriously impacted.

Evaluate, approve, control, and distribute list

The system for evaluation and control of subcontractors can be structured in exactly the same way as the system for suppliers, discussed in the preceding section. It can be based on the same elements:

- subcontractor quality record files containing the initial evaluation records, documents pertaining to the controls exercised over the subcontractors, and the subcontractor approval status sheet; and

- an approved subcontractor list distributed to those involved with requisitions and purchase orders.

The differences between the supplier and subcontractor systems are in the manner and scope of the initial evaluation, and in the means employed for controlling the subcontractor's quality performance.

In addition to the purchasing department, subcontractor evaluation may require the participation of quality

Evaluation may include other departments

assurance, design, and production departments. In fact, in many companies the evaluation of subcontractors is directly assigned to the quality assurance instead of the purchasing department. I personally do not favor such an arrangement, although there are certainly circumstances where it is the best choice.

Purchasing should retain responsibility

In a typical organization, the purchasing department has the primary responsibility for dealing with subcontractors. Taking this responsibility away from purchasing when quality matters are involved can create coordination problems and confusion. Therefore, a a more efficient system is created when the purchasing department retains the responsibility for approval of subcontractors and uses the quality assurance department only as an expert and consultant in the technical aspects of quality evaluation.

Administratively more efficient if purchasing retains control

The subcontractor quality record files can be maintained by either quality assurance or purchasing, whichever is more convenient; but the maintenance of the subcontractor approval status sheet and the approved subcontractor list should be the responsibility of the purchasing department. In fact, if purchasing retains the control of the system, there is no need for distinguishing between suppliers and subcontractors on the administrative level. There will be one system for both but, in the case of subcontractors, the quality assurance, design, and production departments will be called in to make recommendations as technical experts.

Evaluation tools

In addition to the general capacity and quality capability data and references that were required for supplier evaluation, subcontractors can also be asked to fill out quality questionnaires, send in their quality manuals and testing and inspection procedures, provide data pertaining to their process equipment and process capabilities, present samples of similar products, and so forth. When the subcontract is for design or consulting, professional resumes of key personnel may be also relevant.

When to audit the subcontractor

Auditing the subcontractor's quality system is, of course, the most effective way to evaluate their quality capabilities. But auditing is costly for both parties and it should be employed only when the situation merits it. Pre-contract audits are routinely applied when reliability and safety aspects are the primary concern, to include procurement of industrial and military systems, sophisticated machinery and equipment, and contracts for aircraft, ships, offshore oil platforms, etc. In purchasing less important and less critical items, subcontractor auditing may also be relevant if the initial review of the subcontractor's quality capability is inconclusive, or for other reasons, such as a customer's contractual requirement, bad experience with previously used subcontractors, the need to reduce in-house receiving inspection costs, and so forth.

Auditing a specific process

Another consideration when deciding on a subcontractor audit is the certification and/or recognition of the subcontractor's quality system. If their system is certified to ISO 9000 or has been successfully audited by their other major customers, the benefit from yet another audit is questionable, unless there is a compelling reason to doubt the certification and/or the references. However, there is a situation where ISO 9000 certification offers very little assurance: The certification cannot be trusted when the concern is a specific process capability. In this case the subcontractor should be audited, but the scope of the audit should focus exclusively on the concerned process and the verifications of the results of that process.

Request supplier to obtain certification

A comprehensive ISO 9000 subcontractor audit conducted by a customer is costly, disruptive, and often pointless. To give meaningful results, the audit should be conducted by a team of professional auditors engaging the subcontractor's entire organization for a couple of days. The audit is very intrusive and disruptive. If not carried out professionally, it can cause a lot of bitter feelings and bring no real benefits. It is much better to ask the subcontractor to get certified with an independent third-party registrar.

Document subcontractor evaluation system in procedure

Coming back to our principal issue of the ISO 9000 requirement for subcontractor evaluation, the scope of the requested information, participation of other departments, and the policy regarding subcontractor auditing must be documented in a procedure. If the basic system is the same for both suppliers and subcontractors, the procedure can start with an explanation of the system as it applies to suppliers, and then state the additional requirements that apply to subcontractors.

Establish controls for subcontractors

The controls exercised over the subcontractors do not need to be more elaborate than those applicable to suppliers. The supplier quality performance monitoring system, discussed in the preceding section, can be adopted for subcontractors without changes. When applicable, the scope of the controls can be augmented with periodical auditing of subcontractors quality systems and witnessing of in-process and/or final inspections at their premises. The procedure for monitoring subcontractor performance can be structured like the other purchasing procedures: first describe the system as it applies to suppliers and then provide the additional requirements applicable to subcontractors.

Establish approval record and list

There is also no reason to differentiate between suppliers and subcontractors in such matters as the formal approval record, the approved subcontractor list, and grandfathering of existing subcontractors. The *ISO 9000 Documentation* book contains a supplier and subcontractor assessment procedure that illustrates how these functions can be documented.

PURCHASING DATA

Requirements pertaining to purchasing data are very specific

ISO 9000 Section 4.6.3, Purchasing data, contains requirements pertaining to the description of the purchased products and verification of purchasing documents. The section is uncharacteristically specific. It lists precisely what must be included in the purchase orders. Because the requirements are so specific, no interpretation is necessary. This makes it easy to establish, document, and implement a complying system, but it also makes it easy for auditors to find a noncompliance. If a purchase order does not contain one of the required description items, there is not much room for defending it or explaining it away.

Identify product precisely

The standard requires that products be precisely identified — including type, class, and grade — when applicable. When auditors see a generic trade name used on a purchase order and suspect that this is not the formal and full identification of the ordered product, they may ask for the supplier's catalog to check if indeed the full identification would include specifying the type, class, or grade of the product. If confusion is even just a theoretical possibility, there is a noncompliance.

Identify drawings and specifications

Similar methods will be used to verify whether other requirements pertaining to identification of referenced drawings, specifications, and standards are implemented. Missing identification of the revision level of a drawing or a standard is an easy noncompliance to spot.

Identify quality requirements

The next issue is the identification of quality requirements. For more complex or critical custom products, auditors will expect that purchase orders request material certificates, inspection and test reports, qualification of first product, submittal of drawings and/or samples for approval, and so forth. Also, when applicable, compliance with ISO 9000 or other quality system standards should be specified. The purchasing documents should always require compliance with ISO 9000 when addressed to an ISO 9000 certified subcontractor or to those claiming that they have implemented the standard.

Review and verify purchasing requirements

The last paragraph of Section 4.6.3 mandates review and approval of purchasing documents prior to release. At first it may look like every company satisfies this requirement automatically because, regardless of ISO 9000, purchasing documents are normally reviewed and authorized with a signature. The issue is not approval of the financial commitment, however, but the verification of specified requirements.

**Other depart-
ments may need
to review and
approve**

In simple cases when standard catalog products are involved, the same person that reviews the commercial and financial conditions in a purchase order can be instructed to also verify that the description of products is precise and complete and, with one signature, approve both aspects. However, when highly technical custom requirements are specified on purchasing documents, auditors will expect that the design, production, and/or quality assurance departments are also involved in the approval of the purchasing documents prior to release.

Distinguishing between standard catalog products and custom or critical products parallels the division employed for evaluating and monitoring vendors. A coherent quality policy in purchasing should prescribe for a given class of vendors the same level and depth of controls with regard to all activities; i.e., evaluation, qualification, monitoring, and approval of purchasing documents. Thus, if the purchasing department is solely responsible for assessment of suppliers, it can also independently approve supplier purchase orders. When other departments are involved with selecting and monitoring subcontractors, these same departments should also participate in the review and approval of subcontracts.

**Document in
procedure**

The procedure for conducting the review and approval of purchasing documents can be structured in the same way as the procedure dealing with vendor evaluation and monitoring. First, it can describe the basic system for the review of purchase orders for standard catalog products, and then stipulate the additional requirements for subcontractors. For both cases, the procedures must specify the minimum scope of the review, define who is responsible for carrying out the review, and explain how to establish the review records.

8 RECEIVING AREA

Requirements must be implemented regardless of the organization

The receiving function is seldom organized into an independent department. It is usually performed by a functional unit of the purchasing or production departments. The organization is not important; it is the receiving function in the quality system that is being highlighted in this chapter.

The receiving department, which serves as a model in this chapter, has the following responsibilities:

- receiving products and verification of quantities;
- matching received products with corresponding purchasing documents;
- first-stage receiving inspection (visual); and
- product marking or labeling with identification and inspection status.

In most companies the receiving department already does most of these things, but the activities often are not formalized. For example, all shipments usually are inspected visually, but there may be no inspection procedures, no records of the inspections, and the inspected products may not be marked to identify their inspection status.

ORGANIZATION OF THE RECEIVING AREA

Segregate receiving area

As products move from the receiving dock to the storage areas their status will change: from delivered boxes to identified and verified materials and components ready to be used in production. While moving through the identification, verification, and marking processes, the products must be prevented from being used or shipped to customers or subcontractors. This requirement, stated in ISO 9000 Section 4.10.2, Receiving inspection and testing, strongly implies that the receiving area should be segregated from all other areas, especially storage and production.

The ideal: dedicated areas and passage-ways

The ideal layout would be to have a dedicated receiving dock or gate opening directly into an enclosed area for temporary staging of delivered goods. Beyond this temporary staging area, in another enclosed room the shipments are matched with the corresponding purchase orders, the received products are taken out of their boxes, and the first-stage visual inspection takes place. Then, finally, beyond the first-stage inspection area, there would be a quality control laboratory connected by a dedicated passageway with the storage areas. There would also be secured quarantine areas for holding rejected products.

The minimum: segregated receiving area

Not all companies can meet this ideal layout, nor would it be required for all. This type of layout is definitively expected when medical devices, pharmaceutical products, nuclear equipment, or critical application electronics are involved. For less critical products, there may be no need for so many dedicated areas and passageways, but the fundamental principle of segregating the receiving area must be implemented under any circumstances.

Can be segregated by fence or boundary line

When the receiving dock or gate opens directly into the storage areas, or for other reasons receiving is conducted in the storage areas, a partition should be erected (usually a chain link fence). At the very least, a yellow line should be drawn on the floor to separate receiving from storage. The same applies when there is only one gate for receiving and shipping, causing intermingling of these two functions. The gate cannot be divided in two, but the receiving and shipping areas beyond the gate should be separated.

A similar case, although not so common, is when the storage area is far removed from the loading dock and the received products have to travel directly through the production areas. This type of layout is the worst. The received products are often dropped off anywhere between the dock and the stores, and many of them go straight into production without any receiving inspection.

Segregate received products according to their status

Within the receiving area itself there should be dedicated holding and staging locations for goods with different status. Auditors will object to intermingling of products that have just been delivered with products that have passed inspections and are ready to be moved to storage. Rejected products and products that cannot be inspected because certificates or other quality records are missing must be clearly labeled as nonconforming and be moved to a quarantine area.

Establish adequate quarantine area

Quarantines should be within the receiving area or immediately adjacent to it. Preferably, quarantines should be totally enclosed and locked. If the company is not manufacturing critical or regulated products, however, auditors will not insist on secured quarantines. It may be sufficient to dedicate an isolated rack of shelves to be the quarantine area. When quarantine areas are open (i.e., not secured) they should be identified with a sign and every product in the quarantine must be clearly labeled as nonconforming.

Large or heavy items are exempt

Unusually large or heavy items that cannot be easily moved can be exempted from the segregation requirements. These products can be deposited directly in their usual storage locations, or even in the locations where they will be processed. Identification of their status will rely exclusively on labeling. In this situation auditors will expect that the labeling is especially clear and visible and it is well attached to the product.

Another special case is large quantities of materials in bulk or liquids. They are often deposited directly into silos or tanks that may already contain leftover mater-

Bulk materials or liquids also exempt

ial of the same kind. Such materials must either be delivered with recognized certificates, or loads must be held back until the required inspection and testing is completed. Trucks containing loads that have passed the receiving inspection can be provided with green flags, for example, so that when they move onto the dumping ramps or transfer pumps they can be recognized as containing verified material.

Semi-permanent storage is a non-compliance

The receiving and quarantine areas must not be used as semi-permanent storage locations. A very common non-compliance is holding a delivery in the receiving area for a prolonged period of time. Explanations are always credible: The supplier delivered wrong products and then never showed up to take them back; the items are defective but the supplier will not acknowledge it and disputes the charge; or, the purchase order that matches this delivery cannot be found. At issue is not the reason but the length of time. If problems cannot be resolved within three to six months, something must be wrong with the quality management system. In addition to receiving, the investigation of the problem may lead to a noncompliance in the purchasing, production planning, quality control, and quality assurance departments.

RECEIVING INSPECTION

Two-stage receiving inspection

Receiving inspection is discussed in detail in Chapter 11, Quality Control, to include the arguments for and against a two-stage receiving inspection system; wherein standard catalog products are only inspected visually by the receiving clerk, while custom and critical products are additionally subjected to a more technical inspection carried out by quality control. In this section only the first-stage receiving inspection is discussed. Even though inspections are generally the subject of Chapter 11, I decided to discuss the first-stage inspection in this section because it is normally the function of receiving rather than quality control.

The first-stage visual inspection comprises the following elements:

- Identifying products and verifying quantities;

- Checking packages for any signs of tampering or damage;

- Retrieving corresponding purchase orders and verifying that all specified items, including quality certificates and records, have been delivered;

- Visually inspecting products in accordance with a written instruction or a checklist, if applicable; and,

- Marking products and/or packaging with part numbers or other identification and affixing a PASSED label, tag, or stamp. Or, if custom or critical products are involved, moving them to the inspection area for the second-stage quality control inspection.

Receiving performs first-stage inspection

The first-stage receiving inspection, carried out by the receiving clerk, must be documented, recorded, and otherwise controlled in the same formal and strict manner as though the inspection was conducted by quality control. Auditors will expect the scope and depth of these inspections to be defined and documented. The procedure should instruct what to look for, what the acceptance criteria is, and how many items in a batch to inspect. Receiving must also have and use nonconforming material report forms and ON HOLD, PASSED, and REJECTED tags, labels, or stickers.

The inspection record can be established by stamping or signing off a copy of the purchase order. Logs, inspection cards, or other means can also be used. The inspected goods and/or their packaging must be tagged, labeled, or stamped to identify them as having passed receiving inspection. The rules for handling nonconforming products can be the same as for any other type of inspection.

When a two-stage receiving inspection system is used, auditors may ask how the receiving clerk knows which products are custom or critical products, or come from a supplier that is deemed to be unreliable, and must there-

Identify when second-stage receiving inspection is required	fore be further inspected by quality control. To evidence that this aspect is controlled, there should be a system for communicating this information. It could be a code used on the purchase orders, or a list of vendors for each category. If it is a list, it must be established and maintained in accordance with the document control requirements and it must be updated regularly.
Keep open purchase orders current	A serious, but surprisingly common, noncompliance in the receiving area is old and/or obsolete purchase orders in the open (or pending) purchase order file. As an auditor, I could never understand how six months can pass and nobody notices that an ordered product has never been delivered. But it happens once in a while in all companies. If this is discovered without any evidence that there was a follow up, auditors will question the whole procurement system and other elements of the quality system as well. If the investigation of this problem concludes that it resulted from a breakdown of a whole chain of controls, the noncompliance will be very serious.
Keep purchase order changes current	The problem is not so serious (although definitely a noncompliance) if a follow up is in progress, or if the order was canceled but the purchase order file in the receiving department was not updated accordingly. The same applies to change orders. Auditors will try to verify that copies of amendments to purchase orders are promptly transmitted to receiving and that they are filed properly so that it is clear a purchase order was changed.

PRODUCT IDENTIFICATION MARKING

Control methods for marking product	The last issue in this chapter is product identification marking. If receiving is responsible for product marking, auditors will investigate how they are informed what part number or other designation pertains to a given product, and what other marking (traceability) should be applied to the product. The most common method is a computer printout of a parts list. This method is fine, but in practice the lists are often not authorized, are not kept current, and do not comply with other requirements for document control. In preparation for the ISO

9000 audit, the parts lists should be reviewed and brought under the document control system. In companies manufacturing mostly custom products, or where production runs are very short, the part numbers and other marking information can be identified directly on the purchase orders.

Marking methods may need to be documented

The methods and techniques to be used for marking products may need to be documented in work instructions, unless they are usual and obvious. For example, the instructions could explain when to use tags, labels, or paint; how to apply them; and when it is sufficient to mark the packaging or when each individual product must be identified. Chapter 10, Production Departments, contains a section discussing work instructions and the criteria for deciding when work instructions are required.

STORAGE AREAS

Preparing storage areas for compliance may require a major effort

Preparing storage areas for compliance with ISO 9000 often requires a major effort. The evaluation of the storage areas and the plan to bring them into compliance should be developed as early as possible. It is likely that the existing storage areas will have to be reorganized and that some additional storage locations will need to be designated. New systems for receipt, dispatch, inventory management, and identification of stored goods may also be required. It is not unusual for the storage areas to become one of the most time consuming items of the ISO 9000 implementation project.

Storage requirements

Storage areas include not only stockroom or warehouse facilities, but also quarantine, staging, and holding areas. The primary requirements for storage areas are stipulated in ISO 9000 Section 4.15.3 Storage. The section is very short but it contains three distinct requirements:

- Storage areas must be designated — meaning defined, dedicated, authorized and, in some cases, secured;
- There must be a system for authorizing receipt and dispatch of products to and from the storage areas;
- Condition of product in stock must be assessed regularly.

Related storage requirements

In addition to these primary requirements, the storage, quarantine, staging, and holding areas will also be audited against selected requirements from Section 4.7, Control of customer supplied product; Section 4.8, Product identification and traceability; and Section 4.12, Inspection and test status. The requirements apply only to finished products and the materials, components, parts, and subassemblies that are incorporated into the products. Such items as office, janitorial, and maintenance supplies and equipment do not have to be controlled. The control of supplies, tools, and equipment used in production is governed by a different, although somewhat similar, set of requirements discussed in Chapter 10, Production Departments.

FUNCTION AND SEGREGATION

Define and dedicate storage areas

Storage areas must be dedicated and authorized for specific use. Storage locations as well as staging, quarantine, and holding areas must be identified in procedures, and signs should be posted to indicate their function and restriction of access, if applicable. Storage of materials, components, finished products, supplies, tools, etc., outside of the designated areas is a noncompliance.

Segregate goods according to type

One of the basic requirements is functional segregation. Different kinds of goods should not be intermingled in the same storage. This does not mean that certification auditors will not accept materials and components being in the same store with packaging boxes, for example. Auditors understand that smaller companies cannot afford to build a separate store for five different categories of goods. It will, however, be expected that different kinds of items are at least assigned to different aisles, racks, or shelves. Regardless of space constraints, items such as defective goods and scrap may not be stored with new stock.

Pay special attention to finished products

When planning for segregation and assignment of storage areas, special attention should be paid to the storage of finished products. These items have already passed the final acceptance inspection and, from the point of view of the quality system, will not be verified again before they are shipped to customers. Even in relatively small companies it is common to see segregated and secured stores dedicated exclusively to finished products. Such special stores should be established whenever possible, but it is not mandatory. Auditors will not question the arrangement if finished goods are stored in a general purpose store, as long as they are placed in a dedicated area and do not seem to be at risk of damage or deterioration.

Consider other types of storage areas

Quarantines and holding areas for nonconforming items and items awaiting inspection should also be considered when assessing storage areas. While the requirement for segregating different kinds of goods may be somewhat open to interpretation, segregation of items that have a negative or unknown inspection status is mandatory. Secured quarantine areas provide the highest level of protection and are mandatory in companies that manufacture critical or regulated products. In other cases, areas for holding nonconforming and uninspected items comply with ISO 9000 as long as:

- they are formally designated for this purpose;
- they are not in immediate proximity to areas where verified products of the same kind are stored; and,
- they are identified with signs designating their use and restricting access.

Heavy objects, materials in bulk, and other items that cannot be easily moved may be exempted from this requirement for segregation, but they must be contained and clearly labeled as nonconforming.

Secured area vs designated area

The 1987 version of ISO 9000 required that the storage areas be secured. The first sentence of Section 4.15.3 read: "The supplier shall provide secured storage areas or stock rooms to prevent damage and deterioration of product ..." In the 1994 revision of the standard the word *secured* is substituted by the word *designated*. This is a significant improvement and will end the confusion about what the word secured meant. Some auditors interpreted *secured* as a requirement for an enclosed area with a door or a gate that could be locked to restrict access. While such security arrangements are applicable and justified in some cases, it was unreasonable to impose them on every storage area in all companies.

Now the word *designated* is widely interpreted to mean that a storage area must be exclusively dedicated and authorized for its defined purpose and be clearly segregated from adjacent areas. The nature of the segregation is no longer so restrictive.

What is segregation?

The interpretation of segregation can be best illustrated by the case where production-related raw materials and parts are stored directly in the production areas, and where there is no restriction of access. Theoretically, as long as these locations are dedicated, segregated, and there is no apparent risk of the stored items being damaged as a result of the production activities, there should be no objection. But in practice, while such arrangement is in itself acceptable, it may still be indirectly responsible for various kinds of related noncompliances. It is very difficult to control inventory, product and inspection status identifications, and rotation of stock in such dispersed and open storage areas, and auditors will investigate this type of arrangement more thoroughly for noncomplying conditions. If there is evidence of a pattern of mismanagement, they could object to the entire setup.

Every company must decide for itself what the minimum segregation requirements ought to be to ensure adequate protection and control, and be able to convince auditors that the implemented solutions work. Although open storage areas have legitimate applications and should not be discouraged hastily, we all know that a chain link fence or a wall offers the most effective segregation. The fence or wall type of segregation should be provided unless there are prohibitive reasons why it cannot be done.

Avoid high-risk location

On the other hand, there is no doubt that staging and holding areas for products awaiting the next processing stage or an in-process inspection can be located in the production areas and be freely accessible. But these areas must also be dedicated and sufficiently segregated to minimize the risk of damage caused by production activities.

CAPACITY EVALUATION

Where is product
currently stored?

The first step in implementing ISO 9000 in storage areas should be the evaluation of existing conditions against the criteria discussed above. The evaluation should start with listing the types of goods that are being stored in the company and matching them with a list of existing storage areas. The matrix will quickly show the types of goods that are "homeless". They are usually materials purchased long ago for products that have since been discontinued; abandoned shipments for customers who have become insolvent; excess materials left over from production; broken machines and equipment; regraded products that may some day find a customer; and so forth. Trying to assign storage areas for these types of goods is an enlightening experience.

Organizing can
save money

While the primary reason for this exercise is to check if the existing storage capacity is sufficient, it also makes a company aware of what it really needs and uses. The organizing, cleaning, and discarding that follows can be very beneficial. The president of a company I recently audited told me they have reclaimed so much space that just the value of this space fully covered the cost of implementing and certifying the quality system.

Evaluate
temporary
storage areas

A similar evaluation should be conducted for holding areas and quarantines. The type of goods that need to be temporarily held in production areas should be identified. Typically they are deliveries awaiting the receiving inspection; materials and components staged for specific production runs or projects; parts and subassemblies waiting for in-process inspections and finished products waiting for final inspections; and products staged for packaging and shipping. The kinds of products that are normally kept in secured quarantine areas are rejected deliveries; parts, subassemblies, and finished products that failed an inspection; and customer-returned products.

It should not come as a big surprise if the conclusion to the storage capacity evaluation is a significant reorga-

Reorganization and cleanup may be required

nization and cleanup of the storage areas. Most companies, especially smaller ones that maintain a general purpose storage, will reach this conclusion. In some cases new storage areas will have to be created, but generally no additional space is needed. Typically the work will consist of reassigning areas, rearranging items, and discarding scrap and junk. It can be a big job. Decisions on what needs to be done must be made early enough to allow sufficient lead time before the certification audit.

RECEIPT AND DISPATCH AUTHORIZATION

Only acceptable product can be received or dispatched

The requirement for receipt and dispatch authorization is the subject of endless discussion and controversy. It sounds like an administrative measure against theft and uncontrolled usage of materials. While this may be an important concern, it is not directly relevant to the quality system. At issue is not designation of authorized personnel or authorizing documents, such as stock receipt cards or job material requisitions, but rather designation of the product quality status authorizing it to be received in and dispatched from storage areas.

Control stock levels for sales

Also, the quantitative control of product movement to and from storage is important to ensure that the level of stock is controlled. The sales and production planning departments cannot satisfy the ISO 9000 requirements pertaining to their activities if they do not know what the current level of stock is for finished products, materials, and components.

What is authorized for receipt and dispatch?

To satisfy the requirement for receipt authorization, the company's policies and procedures should clearly state that only purchased products that have passed receiving inspection, and subassemblies and finished products that have passed final inspection, can be admitted to storage. Similarly, for dispatch authorization, only products with known and positive inspection status can be withdrawn from storage for use or shipping. Procedures should state also how the inspection status is identified. Receipt and dispatch of products that are not identified by a part number or description should be like-wise prohibited.

Establish inventory system

Quantitative inventory control is not directly required anywhere in the ISO 9000 standard. But, as mentioned above, the stock levels is important information for the sales and production planning departments. Auditors will be alerted and suspicious if there is no stock management system at all. In very small companies, where this may be a problem, I would recommend that a simple inventory control system based on stock cards or a log be established, or that inventories be counted very frequently.

Inventory systems will be audited

If a stock management system exists, it will be audited even though the system is not directly required by ISO 9000. It is therefore advisable that stocks be reconciled before the certification audit to make sure that everything on the shelves is also in the computer, and vice versa. The same applies to systems for control of receipt and dispatch. When purchase orders, shipping bills, material requisitions, or sales orders are used for admitting and releasing products to and from stock, the use of these documents and records should be explained in a procedure, and the system should be fully implemented. Auditors will check the records to verify that the systems are used regularly and consistently.

CONDITION OF PRODUCT IN STOCK

It is a noncompliance if damaged product is found

It is a serious noncompliance when auditors find damaged or deteriorated products in storage areas. If the products deteriorated during storage, it is a clear evidence that either the storage area or its management are inadequate. If a damaged or substandard product was admitted to storage, the problem is even more serious; the investigation will spread beyond the storage area into receiving inspection and, possibly, purchasing.

While auditing the storage areas, auditors will look carefully for any signs of product deterioration and inadequate protection of products. The following conditions will attract their attention and provoke questioning:

Damaged
product

■ Products and packaging showing signs of damage will be investigated, to include: product damage that may have occurred during handling or transportation; deterioration resulting from prolonged storage in inappropriate conditions; or simply dirt and dust accumulating on fine components or finished surfaces. Typical examples of damaged packaging are holes in bags, crushed boxes, or wet or water stained cardboard boxes. While damaged products in storage areas are indisputable noncompliances, damaged packaging will be investigated to determine how the damage occurred and to determine if the products inside are affected.

Inconsistent
product
packaging

■ Different packaging or protection for the same products may also lead to a noncompliance. Most often the problem is when a couple of items are taken from their outer box and placed next to it on the same shelf. Even if there is no apparent risk that these items can be damaged, the questions that arise are what, in fact, is the company's standard practice for storing the items? Why were they taken out of the box, while other items of the same kind were not? Similar questions will be asked when the same kinds of products are purchased from vendors that use very different kinds of packaging that do not provide an equivalent level of protection.

Open containers

■ Opened boxes and containers always attract attention. One opened box of several is acceptable if the remaining items are still adequately protected. But two or more opened boxes containing the same items will be questioned. Opening sealed containers with liquids or chemicals often drastically reduces the shelf life of the products, and auditors will always investigate such containers.

Stacked boxes

■ Inappropriate stacking of boxes or pallets resulting in unstable stacks or obvious damage to packages at the bottom of stack due to weight will probably result in a noncompliance. When boxes are marked with "Do not stack over three high," or equivalent warning, higher stacking is a clear noncompliance, regardless whether there is weight damage or not.

Inadequate product dispensers

■ Dispensing products in bulk or liquid that can cause uncontrolled spillage or contamination must be avoided. Spilled chemicals can potentially contaminate other items in storage or create hazardous conditions. Cross-contamination may be an issue if the same containers, shovels, pumps, or lines are used for dispensing different kinds of products. A related matter is labeling of transfer containers. They must be labeled with the same information as the original container, including expiration date if applicable. When full traceability is required, a batch number or other unique identification must be also transferred.

Assess product before audit

In preparation for the ISO 9000 certification audit, the stocked items should be assessed to identify any damaged or deteriorated products and packaging. If the storage areas need to be reorganized and cleaned up, the identification of damaged items can be done concurrently to utilize the same resources and time for both tasks. Periodical assessment of product in stock is directly mandated in the ISO 9000 standards.

Document procedure for periodical assessment

To comply with this requirement, there should be an operational procedure instructing how and how often the periodical assessment of stock ought to be carried out and how to establish records. Annual assessments are usually sufficient, unless the shelf life of products or other special considerations dictate a shorter period. Although the primary purpose of the assessment is to identify deteriorated items and remove them from stock, they should also be used to evaluate the adequacy of the storage areas; the effectiveness of protective packaging; and the effectiveness of other storage controls prescribed by the quality system. Corrective actions should be requested and implemented when the effectiveness is in question.

Another issue related to deterioration of products is management of stock with limited shelf life. Food, drug, and chemical industries are accustomed to handling such products but, almost without exception, every company stores at least a couple of items from this catego-

Control product with shelf life

ry. In machine industries, for example, O-rings have cost many companies a noncompliance because their storage management systems did not provide for control of expiry dates of the O-rings.

When applicable, expiration dates should be displayed on product packaging and be entered in the inventory system. Regardless of whether the shelf life is formally limited or not, all materials and products that deteriorate over time must be issued in rotation to ensure that the oldest stock is used first. Accordingly, there should be a system that allows for on-the-spot identification of the sequence in which individual shipments were received. This can be done by marking, or special stacking or queuing schemes.

Policies and instructions relating to the management of expiration dates and rotation of stock must be documented. The quality manual should state the policies and generally describe those systems, while the operational procedure governing the management of storage areas should provide for more detailed instructions.

Manage controlled environments

The last topic in this section is storage of items that require controlled environmental conditions, such as frozen or refrigerated products, items that are sensitive to elevated humidity, and materials that should not freeze or be exposed to high ambient temperatures.

Measure and record conditions

Whenever storage requires controlled environmental conditions, these conditions must be measured (using calibrated equipment) and the measurements must be recorded. The most common record keeping method is to maintain a log where measurement results, taken at a predetermined frequency, are recorded. In critical cases, such as frozen foods, the measuring instruments should produce continuous hard-copy records and high/low alarms should be installed for additional protection.

Audit effectiveness and adequacy

When evaluating whether the employed methods for monitoring and recording environmental storage conditions are adequate, auditors consider the nature of the stored goods, the general practice in the given industry and, if applicable, regulatory requirements. The overriding principle is that a continuous record of relevant environmental parameters (usually temperature and/or humidity) is required, when deterioration caused by changing environmental conditions cannot be readily detected.

CUSTOMER SUPPLIED PRODUCT

In companies that manufacture special order products or provide services, customers may want to have their own parts, equipment, or furnishings incorporated into the final product. This is a common situation for building contractors, shipyards, industrial or military systems contractors, and for many types of service companies.

Verify, store, maintain customer supplied products

ISO 9000 Section 4.7, Control of customer supplied product, requires that there be procedures for verification, storage, and maintenance of such products. If a company never receives products from its customers, it should state so in the quality manual, and this will be sufficient to comply with Section 4.7. If customer products are being received, an appropriate procedure should either state that customer products are subjected to exactly the same requirements as purchased products are, or describe how verification, storage, and maintenance of customer supplied products are to be carried out.

Notify customer of loss or damage

Additionally, Section 4.7 requires that loss, damage, and unsuitability of customer supplied products must be reported back to the customer. To comply, the quality manual and/or an appropriate procedure should contain a policy responding to this requirement. If dealing with customer products is inherent in the operation, specific measures for recording problems and informing the customer may need to be documented in a procedure.

IDENTIFICATION OF PRODUCTS AND THEIR INSPECTION STATUS

The systems for product identification and inspection status identification will be discussed in detail in Chap-

Identify all stored product

ter 10, Production Departments, and Chapter 11, Quality Control. At issue in storage areas is implementation. Unidentified and unmarked boxes are a noncompliance. Identification of a product and identification of its inspection status are two different things. Product identification indicates what the product is and correlates the product with the drawings and specifications that define it; and an inspection status indicator indicates whether a product passed all inspections prescribed by the quality plan, including the receiving inspection.

Use a part number or name

A common way to identify a product is to give it a part number or a distinctive name with a model or type number, if applicable. When traceability is required, individual products or batches must be uniquely identified with serial numbers, batch numbers, production dates, or a reference to other documents that contain the traceability records. The product identification must be marked directly on products and/or on their packaging. The identification should not be lost when products are taken out of storage. If products are stored in boxes, crates, or other containers, these should also be marked. The same applies to cabinets, shelves, or drawers used for storing products.

Use an inspection stamp, tag, or label

Inspection status identification must follow the same rules as described above for product identification. It can be a receiving inspection stamp, a tag, or a label. If inspection or testing traceability is required, there should also be a reference to the corresponding inspection record. It is often possible to mark the inspection status identification on the same labels or tags that identify the products. A popular system is to put an inspection stamp directly on part number labels.

10 PRODUCTION DEPARTMENTS

The main set of requirements for production departments is contained in ISO 9000 Section 4.9, Process control. In addition, production must also comply with requirements of sections dealing with document control, product identification and traceability, inspection status identification, control of nonconforming product, product handling, training, and statistical techniques.

Section 4.9 is relatively short — about half a page. Most other sections are at least that long and there are some that are much longer. For example, Section 4.11, dealing with measuring equipment, is three times longer. It may seem strange that such an important area, really the core of the quality system, is addressed in such a short and general section. The reason is because ISO 9000 must retain its universality — be applicable to all kinds of manufacturing and service industries, and all sizes of companies — and it cannot, therefore, be too specific and risk irrelevance when applied to particular cases.

Standards lack specific requirements

Although the reasons are understandable, many customer groups and regulatory agencies are disappointed with the standards because of this general approach and lack of more specific requirements for production. They ask, "What protection can we expect from such phrases as 'suitable equipment', 'suitable environment', 'suitable parameters... are required as appropriate'? Can we rely on third-party auditors to determine what is suitable and appropriate?"

The critics have a point, but there are solutions. The United Kingdom Department of Health adopted ISO 9000 in its Good Manufacturing Practice Guide for Sterile Medical Devices and Surgical Products. The guide reprints the whole standard verbatim and adds 13 pages of supplementary specific requirements below section 4.9 to deal with clean rooms, dress codes, sterilization techniques, and other issues relevant to that industry and its products. This, I believe, is an excellent example of how ISO 9000 can be applied in cases where requirements must be more specific.

Auditors look for reasonable controls

However, when there are no addenda with supplementary requirements, it is indeed up to auditors to determine what is suitable. In making this judgment they will consider the nature of the products involved and the complexity of processes. As a rule, auditors will not question the adequacy of specific control methods and means employed, but rather will limit their investigation to verifying that some reasonable controls are implemented where they are explicitly required in the standard.

THE FIRST IMPRESSION

Before starting an audit, auditors will take a general tour through the company to get a first impression. This impression will set the stage for the whole audit. It would seem that auditors should not be swayed by impressions, but rather seek objective evidence for compliance or lack of compliance in every area. Then, at the end of the audit, they should add up their scorecards and reach a verdict. But it does not happen exactly that way. First, auditors develop an impression and a feel for the whole company or a given department. They then reach their verdict and, finally, collect the evidence to support this verdict. Just kidding, but the truth is somewhere in between.

Ideal vs real environments

Asleep, auditors dream about spacious, well-illuminated buildings with shiny floors, modern production machines, and work stations neatly arranged into continuous production lines. Work instructions are displayed behind glass at every work station, and personnel dresses in impeccably clean, light blue uniforms.

Nothing in those buildings clutters the image of a futuristic production facility. Auditors are, however, realists. When they wake up and go to work they will still give ISO 9000 certificates to less-than-perfect companies. Nonetheless, they expect that their dream be shared by the companies they audit and, at a minimum, they will not be seeing scrap, trash, disrepair, neglect, and indifference everywhere.

**Conditions
to avoid**

Specifically, auditors will become skeptical about the company's ability to control its production when they see conditions like these:

- Chaotic arrangement of production flow and intermingling of unrelated operations in the same area.

- Storage of materials, components, and supplies in unauthorized locations, such as free spaces between machines or work stations, under tables, on top of cabinets, and other such convenient, rather than designated, locations.

- Accumulation of unused, downgraded, or scrapped materials around machines and work stations, and storage of such materials in dark corners, along walls, or other such unauthorized locations.

- Machine parts, tools, and supplies scattered around and intermingled with materials, components, and products.

- Abandoned machines or broken equipment allowed to remain indefinitely in the production areas.

- Obstructed transportation or fire lanes.

- Signs of disrepair or inadequate maintenance of handling and transportation equipment, such as containers, carts, lifts, or cranes.

- Unorganized piles of documents — catalogs, drawings, specifications, or standards — in document stations or office areas.

- Dirty or damaged uniforms and violations of the dress code.

- Leaking roofs, broken windows, and other signs of building disrepair.

- Trash, dirt, poor lighting, excessive noise, inadequate protection from atmospheric conditions, and so forth.

Many of these conditions will directly provoke a non-compliance, especially in cases of unauthorized storage and when there is risk of contamination or deterioration of the product. But even when there are no directly identified noncompliances, these conditions create the impression that the quality system does not work. It is difficult to pass the certification audit when a negative impression sets in from the start.

Many problems are related to storage

The cleanup and possible reorganization of production areas should start early on in the ISO 9000 implementation project, and should be synchronized with the cleanup of the storage areas. Typically, most problems will be related to storage and may best be solved by dedicating specific locations for holding scrap, unused materials, and machine tools and supplies; and designating staging and holding areas for products awaiting the next processing step or inspection. All storage-related issues are discussed in Chapter 9, Storage Areas.

If the product is food, drugs, chemicals, electronic components, or other items that can be easily contaminated or damaged by dirt or dust, cleanliness becomes an important environmental control issue. In this case, there should be written cleaning schedules and logs. If contamination by the cleaning agents is a possibility, the agents and the cleaning methods should be documented in procedures.

PRODUCTION PROCEDURES (WORK INSTRUCTIONS)

Work instructions vs documented procedures

The 1987 version of ISO 9000 required that work instructions be provided, where the absence of such instructions could adversely affect quality. In the new edition of the standards this requirement is retained, but now, work instructions are called *documented procedures defining the manner of production*. I have thought a lot about this change and I am still not certain what it means and how it should affect interpretation. True, many people have difficulty understanding when work instructions are required, but the new expression does not clarify anything in this regard. Maybe elevating work instructions to the status of procedures implies that their format, issue, and distribution should be more tightly controlled. If so, one up for the bureaucrats.

Production department should issue and control work instructions

I will still refer to those documents as work instructions (the new name seems a bit too long) and I will still insist that, when practical, they should be issued locally by the department that uses them, and be expressed in any format that is practical and effective. For example, an instruction affixed to a machine stating: "Do not open the feed valve before temperature reaches 250°F" is much more effective than if the message was written in a procedure and kept in a drawer. Application of ISO 9000 requirements for document control may seem to be more uncertain when dealing with a sign affixed to a machine or a wall than a procedure having a special control page with five signatures, but it can be done. Examples of how to effectively control posted instructions and signs are provided later in this section.

When are work instructions needed?

The principal question in this section is when and under what circumstances auditors expect to see work instructions. There are two cases: regular processes that produce inspectable results; and special processes, the results of which cannot be fully verified by subsequent inspection or testing. In this section only regular processes will be discussed. Special processes must satisfy additional requirements stated in the last three paragraphs of ISO Section 4.9, and they are the subject of the next section.

The answers to these questions determine when work instructions are needed

Regarding regular processes and operations, ISO Section 4.9 a) states that work instructions are required where the absence of such instructions could adversely affect quality. Who decides if lack of instructions could adversely affect quality, and what should be the criteria for making this judgment? The company must make this decision for itself and auditors will respect it, unless it is obvious that there was no decision at all and that the lack of instructions is the result of neglect rather than the conclusion that work instructions are not needed. When deciding for each individual operation or process, the following questions should be answered:

- Is the operation sufficiently simple so that an unskilled person, or a person only generally skilled in the art, could be quickly qualified by a simple demonstration and instruction? Is there always someone assigned to offer such demonstration and instruction when emergency replacement is required? If yes to both, work instructions are not needed.

- Do operator qualification requirements for this position comprise the skills necessary to operate this machine or carry out this operation? Are these qualification requirements documented and are there records demonstrating that our operators are qualified? If yes to both, then instructions are not required, unless, in an emergency, an unskilled person would need to be assigned to the operation.

- Do we provide classroom and/or on-the-job training for this operation? Is this training documented and recorded? If both are yes, then instructions are not required unless, as in the case above, an unskilled person would have to be assigned to the operation in an emergency.

- Are there manufacturer's manuals that completely explain how to operate this machine or computer program? Are these manuals available to the operators? If both are yes, the manuals are considered the work instructions and additional instructions issued by the company are not required.

- Is this a special process? If yes, then work instructions probably will be required (see the next section).

If there are no work instructions...

All these issues can be really expressed by one question: If we do not have work instructions, how can we demonstrate that our operators and their replacements have the necessary skills and know-how to do the job? The answers should point to qualification and training documents and records or on-the-job training, and to alternative instructions, such as manufacturer's manuals, assembly instructions that come with purchased parts, or notes on drawings. Arguments like "Jim has over 10 years of experience doing this job" do not sell very well. The auditors will be quick to reply with, "And how many years of experience will you require if you had to replace him?... Are your qualification requirements documented anywhere?"

Most frequently they are needed for assembly

The need for work instructions comes up most frequently in connection with assembly operations. Tasks, that require special methods and skills (such as alignment of parts, balancing rotating elements, and inserting seals) are expected to be documented in work instructions or procedures unless they are simple and obvious and can be quickly learned. Work instructions are also expected for the operation of more complicated machines, especially those with adjustable performance parameters. If certain processes or tooling works best with specific temperature or speed settings, those parameters should be prescribed. Work instructions should also tell operators how to feed in materials, how to clear lines at the end of a run or when the machine jams, and what to do when the machine is not performing satisfactorily or when it breaks down.

Where unskilled workers are concerned...

While many companies will want to economize on work instructions and will test every operation and work station against the criteria listed above, there are cases where it makes more sense to equip every single work station with work instructions, without any regard to obviousness or training. This approach is recommended for companies that employ large numbers of unskilled workers performing routine production or assembly operations. Work instructions are the only way to preserve a certain minimum level of performance and consistency in cases where there are no initial qualification requirements for newly hired employees and the training consists of just a few hours of instructions and demonstrations. When dealing with a large and fluid work force, even the most basic and simple operations will not always be obvious to everyone.

There are no restrictions on work instruction format

Almost any format for work instructions is acceptable. They can be published standards, equipment manufacturer's operating manuals, internal procedures, instruction sheets, flow charts, data sheets, and notes on drawings and specifications. They can be collected in binders, displayed behind glass on special document stands, hung overhead from ceilings, be posted on walls or machines, and take any other format that the company may choose. Whatever their format, work instructions must satisfy the basic requirements of ISO 9000 Section 4.5, Document control. The two that are especially important are: review and approval of work instructions prior to issue (evidenced by signatures and identification of the issuing authority), and a master list identifying their current revision and placement (a log, for example).

Implementing work instructions is quite simple

Implementation of these requirements is quite simple in a company that already has work instructions. First, each production department should decide which documents fall into the category of work instructions. Then, it should list the documents in a log, naming the authority who approved the document, its date of issue or revision level, and the location(s) where it is placed. Finally, the documents should be identified by the document name, approval sign-off and the date of issue or revision level, using a title page, stamp, or label. Instructions and data sheets that are taped to walls or machines do not even need to be taken down. It is sufficient to affix a label with the required document control information. Once all the existing instructions are formalized, every work station and process should be reviewed to determine if additional work instructions will be needed to satisfy the ISO 9000 requirements.

SPECIAL PROCESSES

Auditors always ask about special processes

It is inevitable that auditors conducting the certification audit will ask which of the production processes are considered by the company to be special processes. Nearly half of ISO 9000 Section 4.9 deals with the special processes and it contains fairly precise requirements that are straightforward to audit. Failure to identify the special processes and implement the applicable requirements is a serious noncompliance that may even result in a failed certification audit.

Define special process

As defined in the standard, special processes are those processes whose results cannot be fully verified by subsequent inspection and testing. More conservative auditors interpret this definition to include those processes that, even though theoretically verifiable at some point, are not inspected or tested at that point and then cannot be verified by the final inspection because the process results have been covered up by subsequent processing. In this definition the words *inspection* and *testing* mean, of course, nondestructive inspection and testing.

Examples of special processes

Examples of special processes are: joining materials by welding, soldering, splicing, and gluing; casting of metals and cements; coating with metals, epoxies, and paints; heat, radiation, and chemical treatments of materials; and many others. Services performed in interaction with a customer — such as in medical care, entertainment, or travel — are also considered to be special processes. These examples are only indicative. When identifying the special processes, every process should be analyzed on its own merits. Casting, for example, is generally considered to be a special process because voids and undesirable material characteristics can develop during solidification. However, when the material is clear glass, verification by visual inspection is still possible.

Identify special processes and consider the control elements

The first step in implementing the special process requirements is to assign the production department or, even better, the quality assurance department to identify and draft a list of these processes. Next, each special process should be reviewed to determine how it is currently controlled and if the controls are sufficient to satisfy the ISO 9000 standards. There are four elements of process control:

- written process procedures,
- operator training,

- process and equipment qualification, and

- continuous process monitoring.

The standard does not state precisely which of these four elements are required as the minimum for all cases. The general consensus among auditors is that written procedures and qualified operators are the two elements that are almost always indispensable, regardless of the circumstances.

The choice of process controls will depend on the process itself. If it is a manual or semi-manual process requiring special skills, the emphasis will be on operator qualification. If it is an automatic process performed by a complex machine, the equipment qualification (capability, setting and calibration) will be the key. For a continuous process, a continuous monitoring of process parameters will be appropriate. Process qualification, i.e. destructive testing of specimens, is applicable when there are specified performance characteristics resulting from the process; for example, strength of a joint, adhesion strength of a coating or paint, resistance to chemicals or other adverse environmental conditions, and so forth. The choice is the company's to make and auditors will seldom challenge it, unless it is obviously dictated by convenience alone.

It is unlikely that there are no special processes

Applying the criteria above, a majority of manufacturing companies should be able to identify some special processes in their production. It is not a good idea to tell the auditor that there are no special processes employed in the company unless, even using the most conservative interpretation of the definition, none can be classified as special. The risk is that the auditor will take it upon himself to find these processes. If found, the resulting noncompliance will be much more serious than if just inadequate controls were applied to an otherwise identified special process. In the rare cases where there are no special processes, the operating procedure dealing with process control should state it clearly and declare that, if any special processes are introduced in the future, they will be controlled by operator, equipment, or process qualification and process monitoring, as appropriate.

Document special process controls and instructions

On the documentation level, a separate operational procedure or a section in the general process control procedure should be dedicated to special processes. The procedure should contain a definition of the special process as interpreted by the company, the assignment of responsibility for identification of these processes, and either policies or guidelines, or specific requirements for controlling them. Procedures for qualifying and performing each individual special process should be also be established. These procedures will be normally issued on the third level — the work instructions level — of the quality system documentation.

Record control elements and performance

Every special process control element and its performance must be recorded. Operator qualifications can be evidenced by education diploma, training records, and external or internal certifications. Equipment qualification is normally evidenced by the performance data specified in manufacturer's manuals, a capability test report, or calibration certificates, when applicable. Process monitoring is evidenced by the charts or logs used for recording variations of the controlled process parameters. Process qualification will most often be recorded in a report analyzing the destructive testing results of a specimen. The specific process procedures must clearly state what records are required to evidence the process capability, qualification, and performance.

PRODUCT HANDLING AND PRESERVATION

To prevent damage and deterioration

Product handling is addressed in ISO 9000 Section 4.15.2, Handling. It is probably the shortest and most nonspecific section in the whole standard. It states that the supplier (your company) shall provide methods of handling products that prevent damage and deterioration. Section 4.15.5, Preservation, is not much longer and is just as nonspecific. It requires that appropriate methods for preservation shall be applied. Product handling and preservation would not merit a separate section in this chapter — the issues are obvious — but for the fact that documented procedures are required.

Special handling usually not required

In most companies, products do not require any special handling and preservation techniques. Typically, materials, components, and products are held in bags, bins, or boxes, or are placed on pallets, and are transported around the storage and production areas on trolleys, carts, or platforms, or by forklift trucks. Heavier items can be lifted and transported by cranes.

Usual issues are containers and equipment

If handling operations are just as simple as those described above, the only issues related to handling are maintenance of containers and transportation equipment, and training of crane and forklift truck operators. Bags, bins, boxes, and pallets for holding products should not be damaged or broken, and should be regularly cleaned. The same applies to trolleys, carts, and other transportation equipment. Cranes, hooks, slings, and shackles must be labeled with their maximum safe load capacity, and all the lifting equipment should be inspected annually.

More rigorous requirements for cranes

Where large cranes are used and heavy lifting is a routine operation, auditors will expect a whole system of controls and written procedures regulating the certification, inspection, maintenance, and operation of cranes. Although operation of cranes is normally subjected to workplace safety regulations, it is also relevant to safety of products. I have seen a $2-million tunnel boring machine fall from a crane because home-made hooks cut from a steel plate were used instead of certified crane hooks. Nobody was hurt, but the tunnel boring project was delayed by three months.

Train equipment operators

Crane and forklift truck operators should be designated and trained. A list of authorized operators and their training records are sufficient evidence to convince auditors that the operation of cranes and forklift trucks is controlled. The training can be simple on-the-job instruction, but it must be evidenced by a record (see Chapter 14.)

Normal handling procedures

The procedure governing the handling operations does not need to be very elaborate or even specific, unless special handling techniques are involved. It should mention that containers, transportation, and lifting equipment are maintained in good condition and that equipment operators are trained; and name the authority responsible for implementation and enforcement of these policies.

Preserve products

Preservation of products in storage and throughout production can be addressed in the same procedure. If no special preservation techniques are used, the procedure can just mention segregation, clean and dry storage conditions, and adequate packaging as the means employed for preservation of products.

Document special handling procedures and instructions

If a company uses special handling and preservation techniques, they should be mentioned in the operational procedure and then described in detail in appropriate work instructions. Every company knows what special handling and preservation techniques apply to its products. It can be the use of gloves, electrostatic mats, specially coated tanks or containers, control of temperature and/or humidity, special protective packaging, and so forth. In addition to work instructions, it is sometimes relevant to post signs warning against inappropriate handling of special products.

PRODUCT IDENTIFICATION

Maintain identification throughout production

Requirements of ISO 9000 Section 4.8, Product identification and traceability, must be implemented throughout all stages of production, from the receipt of materials and components through to the dispatch of the finished products. The section starts with the words "where appropriate", indicating that there may be some cases where product identification is not required. In practice, auditors will only accept an unidentified product when it moves through automatic or continuous processing, or when the product is held in an area dedicated exclusively for one kind of product.

Exceptions are discouraged

Auditees often dispute the requirement for identification when recognition of a product is obvious. But the arguments are usually not convincing. Products similar in appearance can be different types, models, or grades; and the ability to recognize them is usually subjective, based on experience. Besides, the requirement for identification is often disputed when the auditor points out an unidentified product type in an area where most other products are identified. This inconsistency betrays the fact that the lack of identification is not the result of a predetermined policy, but rather results from the lack of any policy at all. Thus, if a company elects to let certain products be unidentified at certain production stages, it must be a conscious decision that logically ties in with the whole product identification system.

Identification can be part number or name

Assignment of a part number is the most common way to identify materials and components. Standard stock items, such as bolts, screws, basic construction materials, or generic chemicals can be identified by their trade names and qualified with the size and/or type, if applicable. Auditors will never question the identification names or numbers as long as they are unique and are used consistently. The trade names and part numbers marked on materials and components should be the same as those used on drawings, bills of materials, work orders, and other design output documents.

Identify individually or by accompanying work order

Products or batches of products moving through production processes can be identified by their work orders or job numbers. If products are accompanied by a work order (see Chapter 6), the individual products do not need to be marked or labeled. Otherwise, if the work orders are kept in a central location, the work order number should be labeled on the products or on the containers holding them. When needed, the work orders can then be retrieved to provide the full technical identification.

Identification of finished products is rarely an implementation problem. Companies usually take good care to clearly identify the products they ship to customers. Commercial reasons demand it. In practice, the only cases of noncompliance are when a contract specifies a particular way of identification or marking and the requirement is not followed. On the other hand, the documentation describing the finished product identification system is not always satisfactory.

Document procedures and instructions

The product identification system must be fully documented. Procedures and work instructions should explain who is responsible for assigning part numbers, how they are generated and controlled, what the correlation is between a part number and the technical documentation defining the part, and how part numbers are marked on products or their packaging. When coded numbers are used, the meaning of every group of numbers or letters in the code should be explained.

Evaluate existing identification system

In most, if not all, companies there are existing product identification systems and procedures describing them. In preparation for the ISO 9000 audit the systems should be reviewed to ensure that they are coherent and are consistently used. The procedures may also need to be modified. While the technical aspects of product identification and marking are usually well documented, there is often lacking a more general procedure regulating the system as a whole. Specifically, assignment of responsibilities, methods of control (part lists, indexes, logs, etc.), and correlation with technical documentation and other systems used in the company. The general procedure can be issued on the level of operational procedures, while the technical aspects, such as the meaning of specific codes, rules for generating part numbers for particular lines of products, or product marking techniques, can be classified as work instructions.

Avoid exceptions

To avoid any problems during the ISO 9000 certification audit, every single piece of material, component, subassembly, product, or batches of these items must be identified. Exceptions are discussed at the beginning of this section, but I do not recommend exempting any products without a good reason. When they see an unidentified item, auditors are sure to stop and pull out their note pads. Explanations will sound like lame excuses unless a coherent and documented policy supports the arguments.

The identification system often breaks down in the situation where standard stock hardware, such as bolts or washers, or other small components are taken out of stock and are distributed to work stations. Large quantities of a component may be held in storage in a box or a bin labeled with their part number, while the individual components are not marked. When some of the components are taken out, they are no longer identified.

Maintain identification on small parts taken from stock

This problem may be solved by introducing plastic bags or other transfer containers that can be labeled either permanently or every time they are used for transferring components. A quantity of pre-printed labels placed in a pocket attached to a bin containing components, and a roll of plastic bags hanging in the vicinity, is a practical example of such a system. It is a simple matter to pull out a label and put it into the plastic bag when taking out the components.

Maintain identification when removed from container

A similar problem arises when components are delivered to a work station. They are then usually taken out of the labeled transfer container and are placed on the workbench, thereby losing their identification. In this case a practical solution would be to either leave the components in the transfer container or deposit them on an identified tray, instead of the bare bench.

I do not want to suggest that these two examples of identification loss during the transfer of small components will be noted as a noncompliance in every case; but in situations where different components can look very similar, as electronic components sometimes do, even a temporary loss of identification can become an issue.

Re-label recycled containers

Another common problem is labeling of containers that are reclaimed for holding a different item and are re-labeled for this reason. The old labels should be removed or completely crossed out before the new labeling is applied. A container displaying two different part numbers is a noncompliance. If one or two containers are found, auditors will probably not make an issue out of it. If the problem is more general, it will definitely be noted as a formal noncompliance.

TRACEABILITY

Most traceability systems are voluntary

ISO 9000 does not require traceability. Section 4.8 states that procedures explaining traceability systems must be established only where it is a specified requirement. Traceability can be specified by the customer, by a regulatory body or agency, or it can be a voluntary system specified internally. Contrary to popular belief, most traceability systems are established voluntarily by manufacturers to help with managing their quality systems and servicing their products.

When traceability is required...

Specification of the traceability requirement is not always stated directly. Traceability may be a necessity for some design requirements. For example, if a design calls for material with certain minimum strength or other characteristics and every batch of the material must be tested to verify that it meets these requirements, the material used in production must be traceable to the test certificates evidencing its suitability. Steel used for critical applications is always subjected to testing, and thereby traceability is an implied requirement.

Another example of an implied traceability requirement is when the manufacturer must be prepared for recalling its products from the market. This is most relevant in food, drugs, medical devices, automotive and other industries manufacturing products that can be potentially hazardous to the public. Without traceability records it would not be possible to determine which batches or series of products should be suspected and recalled.

However, these cases are the exceptions. Most companies maintain traceability systems not because of stated or implied requirements from customers or regulatory bodies, but because traceability helps with investigating quality problems and implementing corrective actions. Also, traceability is very helpful in servicing complex mechanical or electrical equipment, such as machines or computers.

Voluntary systems are vulnerable to noncompliances

Voluntary traceability systems are the most vulnerable to an ISO 9000 audit because they are often poorly defined and documented and are not consistently implemented. I do not want to discourage companies from maintaining voluntary traceability systems. On the contrary, auditors recognize them as an indication of the importance of quality in a company. But when nobody in the company is sure which materials, components, or processes are being traced; when the traceability records are not properly maintained; and when there is evidence that the traceability system breaks down at various operations, auditors will be less impressed and, even though it is a voluntary system, will not hesitate to note the noncompliances.

Evaluate existing system

All companies should review their traceability systems in preparation for the ISO 9000 certification audit. Problems with traceability are so common that no company should risk presenting its system for the audit before first checking it. To do a thorough check, first review the bills of materials, parts lists, and processes. Flag those items on the lists for which traceability is required. Then, for every traceable item, check if the methods employed for assuring traceability, such as segregation and labeling, are effective through all storage and production stages. Finally, review the corresponding traceability records for completeness and consistency. This is exactly what the auditors will do, except they will investigate only a sample, not all items.

Maintain traceability on parts

Problems with maintaining traceability are similar to those associated with the maintenance of product identification. In fact, the only difference is that in the case of traceability the identification is unique to each product or batch, while product identification is the same for all products of the same kind. Consequently, the preceding section discussing the maintenance of product identification is directly applicable to the maintenance of traceability, and should be consulted in this regard.

Traceability is often lost when a portion of material is cut away, as in a piece of pipe or plate, or when bulk or liquid material is taken from a container or a tank. In the case of material that needs to be cut, the cut-out piece should immediately be marked with the unique identification, such as a purchase order number, which links it to the associated records. For partial transfer of bulk or liquid material, the most obvious method is labeling the transfer containers.

Another kind of problem with maintenance of traceability arises when a couple of items are taken from a batch for rework. In many cases the loss of productivity that would result if the whole batch was to be held back until the defected items are reworked is unacceptable, and establishing a new traceability record for just a few items is also considered too costly. What happens in these cases is that the reworked items are either incorporated into a batch that happens to be near by, or they are bunched together into one "batch". This sounds like a joke, but it really does happen. I do not have any ready solutions. Every situation has its specific circumstances that must be taken into consideration and dealt with as best as possible.

Establish traceability record

The additional element in a traceability system that is not present in a product identification system is the traceability record. An excellent vehicle for the traceability record is the work order that accompanies a product or a batch of products through all production phases. If the scope of traceability is extensive, a separate special form can be attached to the work order. As materials and components are taken out of stores and the product moves from one processing stage to another, the unique identification of the materials, components, and processes can be recorded on the work order. This can be done by the employees responsible for issuing materials or operating process equipment. The use of the work order for this purpose was discussed in Chapter 6, Production Planning.

Document traceability procedures and instructions

ISO 9000 requires that the whole traceability system be documented in procedures. This can be done on several levels. An operational procedure should describe the system as a whole and state the general policy outlining the scope and depth of traceability. Drawings, work orders, or special traceability forms can name the specific items and processes for which traceability is required. And, in addition, if the marking of products or establishing traceability records is not obvious, work instructions should be issued for these activities.

INSPECTION STATUS IDENTIFICATION

Inspection status must be identified and maintained

It is usually not the responsibility of production departments to establish the identification of product inspection status. In this book I assume that this is a function of quality control. Accordingly, the main discussion of the related issues will be included in Chapter 11, Quality Control. The relevant aspect in this section is the maintenance of the inspection status identification throughout production.

...As in product identification

The 1994 revision of ISO 9000 is more strict than the initial 1987 issue of the standard. Maintenance of the inspection status identification is no longer optional, and must be now applied to all materials, components, and products throughout all stages of production. Exceptions can still be considered in some cases, and they are also discussed in Chapter 11.

The systems, methods, and potential problems associated with the maintenance of inspection status identification are very similar to those discussed earlier for product identification and traceability. In fact, the methods are exactly the same: product marking, tagging or labeling, or accompanying the product with a work order. The same tags, labels, or work orders that are used for product identification can be stamped with inspection stamps to identify the inspection status of products.

Products that fail an inspection must be identified by a more visible means. Usually, a large red ON HOLD or

Identify noncon-forming product

NONCONFORMANCE tag or label is used for this purpose, and the nonconforming products are segregated. In regulated industries it may be also required to place nonconforming products in secured quarantine areas.

Possible exception for receiving inspection

As is the case with unidentified products, a noncompliance will result for every product that is found without an identification of its inspection status. When the receiving inspection status identification is the issue, the noncompliance is less serious and can be argued. If all materials and components are labeled with their status identification when in storage, an argument can be made that loss of identification when the items are taken out of storage does not matter because the only way materials and components can enter production is by being checked out of storage. The standard does not explicitly allow for any exceptions, but auditors may go along with this argument.

Identification mandatory through all other stages

On the other hand, the lack of inspection status identification on products moving through production operations is a clear noncompliance unless there are no in-process inspections. The most serious problem is when auditors find a finished product ready for dispatch without any identification that it passed the final inspection. Final inspections are always mandatory and there are no arguments that can be made in defense of this situation.

PRODUCTION EQUIPMENT MAINTENANCE

Production equipment always audited

Production equipment maintenance is one of those activities that auditors never fail to audit, even though it is addressed in the standard by only one nine-word sentence. The sentence is the last item of production control elements listed in Section 4.9. It simply states that production equipment must be maintained to ensure continuing process capability.

Repairing break-downs is not maintenance

Because there is no mention of procedures, maintenance plans, logs, records, or any other specific suggestions for what should be included in the equipment maintenance system, every company must decide for itself what it needs to do. The only option not available is to do nothing. Whatever the system, it must have elements of preventive maintenance; the words "to ensure continuing process capability" strongly suggest that repairing breakdowns is not enough to satisfy the requirement.

Minimum components of maintenance system are assignment of responsibility, a plan, and a record

In a credible equipment maintenance system there must be a person or a department assigned with the responsibility to carry out the maintenance, a maintenance plan, and a record evidencing what maintenance servicing has been performed for each machine. In a small company with relatively simple equipment the system does not need to be very elaborate. The person assigned with the responsibility to maintain the equipment may be a machinist, for example, who normally works in production. The maintenance plan can be a simple list or a matrix specifying how often oil, seals, drive belts, and other supplies and parts need to be changed or replaced for each machine. The equipment manufacturer's servicing manuals can be also shown to auditors as the evidence that preventive maintenance requirements are defined. The maintenance record can be a simple log for recording repairs and maintenance servicing.

More complex equipment requires more detailed system

The system described above represents just the basics. Something more substantial will be expected in larger companies with complex machines and equipment. While the elements are still the same, i.e. responsibility assignment, maintenance plan, and maintenance records, each should be more developed. Qualifications of mechanics should be documented, every piece of equipment should have its own file containing a detailed maintenance plan and maintenance records, and periodical inspections and testing of equipment should be prescribed.

Briefly describe maintenance system in general procedure

Although Section 4.9 does not explicitly require any procedures for the equipment maintenance system, it is advisable to mention in an operational procedure for production control that such a system exists. A section of the procedure can briefly describe the preventive maintenance system and provide general instructions for equipment operators to protect and maintain their equipment on a daily basis and to promptly report any symptoms of malfunctioning to those responsible for equipment servicing.

ENVIRONMENTAL CONDITIONS

Generally, it is a level of cleanliness

Most industries do not control environmental conditions in their production areas except for maintenance of a general level of cleanliness appropriate to the type of manufactured products. If this is the case, the only thing that needs to be done is to clean up the production areas and include a couple of sentences in the quality manual or an operational procedure stating that cleanness is an important prerequisite for quality and that production areas are regularly cleaned.

When control is necessary a complete system is required

In industries where processes require specific temperature and/or humidity levels, or the requirement for cleanness is stated in terms of allowable biological burden and/or particulate levels, a complete environmental control system, including procedures, monitoring instruments, and records, must be established. The principles of any environmental control system are:

- that the maximum and/or minimum allowable levels of the controlled parameter are defined and documented;
- that a calibrated instrument or an approved testing method is used to monitor the level of the parameter;
- and that a record of the level of the controlled parameter is produced continuously or is established at regular time intervals.

Monitor conditions with calibrated instruments and record results

In practice, when the controlled parameter is temperature and humidity, a calibrated thermometer and hygrometer should be placed centrally in the controlled area and a sign (controlled document) stating the maximum and/or minimum allowable levels of temperature and humidity should be displayed next to the instruments. If the instruments are equipped with dial charts or other means for tracing a continuous record, the charts should be regularly reviewed and filed as a record.

If the temperature and humidity readings are recorded manually, the time interval between readings must be defined and a specific person must be designated to do it. Documentation of this function can be issued as a work instruction and be placed in the vicinity of the instruments together with the records log.

Investigate out-of-tolerance condition

When an out-of-tolerance reading of the temperature or humidity is observed, an investigation should follow to determine the extent of the damage to the processed products and an appropriate decision should be made to accept, rework, or scrap the products. In addition, a corrective action should be proposed and implemented to avoid recurrence of the problem that caused the temperature or humidity to deviate from the specified tolerance.

Test conditions for control

Control of particulate level and biological burden is more complicated. There are no instruments that can directly measure their values. Tests used to determine these values must be documented in procedures and be carried out at prescribed time intervals. Additionally, strict preventive measures must be implemented and monitored to assure that the particulate level and the biological burden stay under the specified limit.

Control the environment and the preventive measures

Such measures will typically include maintaining overpressure in the production areas, filtering of air, strict dress code and hygiene requirements, special cleaning techniques, use of air locks and sticky mats, transferring products into the area in double bags, and many other techniques known to industries operating clean rooms. If the control of particulate level and biological burden is critical, as in the drugs and medical devices industries, an elaborate system of procedures, records, and traceabilities is required, not only for controlling the environment itself, but also for controlling each preventive measure employed to ensure that the environment complies with the specified limits.

The control of temperature, humidity, particulate level, and biological burden discussed in this section is by no means an exhaustive list of environmental parameters that may need to be controlled. Every company knows what specific parameters it must control, and should use the above examples as an indication of what ISO 9000 auditors will expect of an environmental control system.

Environmental protection for people?

Another concern is the environment affecting people employed in production. Auditors normally do not issue formal noncompliances when products are not at risk, but they do not fail to notice such conditions as inadequate ventilation, excessively high or low temperatures, poor lighting, unbearable noise, and so forth. I once issued a noncompliance for a leaking roof, although I classified it as being a potential hazard to the products rather than discomfort to the employees. ISO 9000 protects products, not people.

OTHER REQUIREMENTS

In the preceding sections I discussed all the major activities pertaining to production that, in most companies, need to be reviewed, established, and implemented in preparation for the ISO 9000 certification audit. However, ISO 9000 Section 4.9 also contains other requirements that have not yet been mentioned. I do not feel that they deserve separate sections because they are so basic. In a properly managed company they are always implemented. These requirements are:

- Use of suitable production equipment;
- Compliance with standards, quality plans, and procedures;
- Monitoring and control of process parameters and product characteristics; and
- Stipulation of criteria for workmanship.

Obtaining evidence of noncompliance is difficult

Compliance with these requirements is difficult to audit. They are stated in such a general manner that the auditee can always argue that he satisfies them or that they do not apply in his company. Auditors are not going to request that new equipment be purchased because the current equipment is old and they suspect that it may be out of tolerance. To make such an assertion, auditors must have solid evidence that the equipment is not suitable. Control of process parameters and stipulation of workmanship criteria presents a similar problem. Auditors will only request evidence of implementation of these ISO 9000 requirements when there is evidence that processes are malfunctioning or that the quality of workmanship is unacceptable.

Auditors do not employ extreme measures

There are, of course, ways to verify suitability of equipment, process stability, or quality of workmanship. But, to check equipment or processes it may be necessary to shut down production and conduct tests that can take hours or even days to complete. Auditors will never employ such extreme methods to prove their point and, besides, there is no time during the audit for such in-depth investigations. Consequently, the benefit of doubt goes to the auditee.

Evidence may be by happenstance

There are also situations when auditors stumble into evidence without looking for it. Evidence of broken or damaged tools, a heat treatment process where the temperature is not being recorded, or series of products with apparent excessive variation in workmanship quality between individual items will undoubtedly provoke a noncompliance.

Process monitoring systems must be complete

While the need for process control can be difficult to prove, those process monitoring systems that are implemented are just as vulnerable to a noncompliance as any other system. Companies that carry out statistical process control must do it properly. Procedures should instruct what data ought to be collected and at what intervals, and which statistical techniques should be used to analyze the data. Mere collection of data and charting is not sufficient. Someone has to statistically process the data and compare the results against defined benchmarks. If the results are not satisfactory, corrective actions should be proposed and implemented. Too many companies have files full of control charts, but there is no evidence that anything other than filing is done with them.

Indicators of an inadequate system

If process monitoring is not documented in procedures, it is not applied consistently, data are not analyzed, there are no benchmarks, or corrective actions are not implemented to follow up on deviations, auditors will issue a noncompliance without hesitation — and it will be a serious one. Such deficiencies are not just mistakes, but an indication of an inadequate system.

Workmanship standards must comply with document control

Workmanship standards, as with any standards, whether they are written specifications, photographs, or actual samples, must comply with the requirements for document control. Although a sample does not physically resemble a document, it should be processed and handled as such. Its identification, authorizing release signature, and a revision number should be displayed on a tag or a sticker, and the same information should be entered into a log maintained by the department that issued the sample.

11 QUALITY CONTROL

There are two chapters in this book that deal with quality functions: this chapter and Chapter 16, Quality Assurance. Most companies have only one department concerned with quality and do not distinguish between quality control and quality assurance. Organizing this book by dividing the quality functions is not meant to suggest that companies should have two departments dealing with quality; rather this chapter about quality control is a follow up to the previous chapter about production and it discusses product verification techniques. The chapter addressing quality assurance is at the end of the book and it discusses quality functions that pertain to the whole quality management system, namely internal audits and corrective actions.

Quality control vs quality assurance

The terms *quality control* and *quality assurance* are often used interchangeably to denote all quality functions. There is, however, a difference between their meanings. Paraphrasing the definitions given in ISO 8402, Quality Vocabulary, *quality assurance* is all actions necessary to provide confidence that quality requirements will be satisfied, while *quality control* is the operational techniques used to fulfill requirements for quality. Practical interpretation of these definitions is that quality assurance is the management and administrative functions of a quality system, and quality control is the operational functions. Accordingly, only the operational functions of the quality system, namely product verification, identification of nonconforming product, and establishment of quality records, will be discussed in this chapter.

Product verification is the key

Product verification is at the core of the ISO 9000 series of standards. The lowest common denominator is the ISO 9003 standard dealing exclusively with final inspection and testing. ISO 9002 and 9001 add on other quality control and quality assurance functions, but they still put the emphasis on product verification activities. The standards are sometimes criticized as being conservative and outdated in this respect, and they conflict with some TQM models that advocate the abolishment of inspections and testing. The critics may be right, but the standards are intended for general worldwide acceptance and not as experimental quality system models.

No alternatives to an inspection and testing system

Those companies that for any reason do not want to implement a clearly defined inspection and testing system probably should not apply for the ISO 9000 certificate. Auditors do not accept alternative methods that bypass inspections; regardless of how effective they may be, they are not mentioned in ISO 9000.

QUALITY PLAN

What is a quality plan?

All ISO 9000 sections dealing with verification of products require that inspecting and testing shall be carried out in accordance with the quality plan and/or documented procedures. The quality plan is often mentioned in the standard, but there is no clear explanation of what it is. I have examined all references to the quality plan in both the old and new revisions of the five ISO 9000 standards and ISO 8402, Quality Vocabulary, and have concluded that every one of these documents propose a different interpretation of a quality plan. On the one extreme, ISO 9004 (1987) implies that the quality plan is the entire quality management system, and on the other extreme, ISO 8402 defines it as a document setting out specific quality practices and activities for a particular product.

Auditors generally adopt the definition given in ISO 8402 (ISO 9000 also references this standard) and, when asking for a quality plan, they mean the program for

Every type of product must have its own quality plan

receiving, in-process, and final inspections and testing relevant to a particular product. Although the definition in ISO 8402 suggests that the quality plan is a document, everyone agrees that the plan can be referenced in many different documents, such as drawings, specifications, work orders, or procedures. The note at the end of ISO 9000 Section 4.2.3, Quality planning, supports this interpretation.

Plan the receiving, in-process and final inspection and testing

Every particular product or type of product must have its own quality plan. The plan defines at what stages — starting from receipt of materials and components and ending on the last operation or process — the product is inspected or tested; and stipulates the scope and manner of each inspection or test and the form of the required record. Those inspections that are common for all types of products (for example, receiving inspection) can be documented in a general procedure, while in-process and final inspections specific to a particular product can be documented in the work order, special inspection instructions, or by reference to inspection notes on drawings.

Document the quality plan

For a typical manufacturing company I recommend the following system for documenting the quality plan:

- Receiving Inspection: A general operational procedure defining the scope and manner of inspections for different classes of materials and components; and, where applicable, work instructions explaining the relevant inspection techniques and acceptance criteria.

- In-process Inspection: A general operational procedure explaining the system; a work order calling out specific in-process inspections; and, where applicable, work instructions explaining inspection techniques and acceptance criteria.

- Final Inspection: A general operational procedure; a checklist specifying all records and aspects of the product that must be verified; and, where applicable, specific inspection instructions and acceptance criteria.

Know what the quality plan is and where to find it

Whether the system described above is followed or not, the quality assurance manager or anyone escorting auditors must know how the quality plan is documented. I often see consternation and puzzled faces when I ask auditees for the quality plan. Not knowing what the quality plan is, in itself will not be a noncompliance. But quality plans are mentioned in so many places in ISO 9000 that auditors will wonder how the company could understand and implement the standards without knowing what a quality plan is.

RECEIVING INSPECTION

All products must be verified upon receipt

No matter how hard we analyze the ISO 9000 standard, or how much we twist and turn the sentences and words of Section 4.10.2, Receiving inspection and testing, the conclusion is always the same: Every product received must be inspected or otherwise verified. When I made this statement while auditing a construction site, the superintendent looked at me disbelievingly and asked, "Do we really have to inspect all the nails, bricks, and paint that are delivered to the site?" I am not sure if those involved with writing and publishing the ISO 9000 standards have ever seen a construction site, but I know from experience that, to satisfy the requirement for receiving inspection, many companies have to be creative if they do not want to hire an extra inspector to look at nails and bricks.

Appropriate interpretation of the requirements is essential

On the other hand, there are industries (such as chemical and pharmaceutical) where companies maintain sophisticated laboratories dedicated exclusively to inspecting and testing purchased materials and components. Those laboratories are there, not to impress auditors, but because they are really needed. A small contractor and a large pharmaceutical company must both comply with the same ISO 9000 standard. An appropriate interpretation of the requirements is therefore crucial to successful implementation.

There are cases when receiving inspection may not be meaningful or even feasible. Sterile products cannot be taken out of their packaging before use; tampering with packaged products intended for resale is not advisable; and not much can be gained from opening a can of paint. Of course, the contractor who buys three cans of paint could send samples of the paint for analysis to an accredited laboratory, or witness the final inspection of the paint at the manufacturer's plant. But not everybody is willing to go to such extremes for an ISO 9000 certificate.

Never say "we do not inspect..."

Although auditors know that the requirement for receiving inspection cannot be implemented in some cases, and in many others the benefit is minimal at best, the words "we do not inspect . . ." must never be uttered during a certification audit. The three cans of paint are, of course, inspected. When they are delivered to the construction site, the foreman verifies that it is the right kind and color of paint. He examines the cans carefully for any signs of damage and checks if the lids are tight and have not been tampered with. Shaking the cans assures that the paint is liquid and, if everything is in order, PASSED stickers are affixed to the lids before the paint is released to his people.

No realistic person will expect that this procedure for inspecting paint will be implemented consistently, except maybe for affixing the PASSED stickers. But as long as the procedure is documented and PASSED stickers are in fact applied, auditors will not investigate further, satisfied that they do not have to argue with the contractor about the need for inspecting the received paint. The fact that the product itself — the paint in the can — was not inspected, will not be challenged.

Critical or custom products must be properly inspected

While the inspection methods described above can be used when relatively small quantities of noncritical standard products are involved, auditors will not be lenient when important materials or components are not being properly verified before use. The example of the three cans of paint should not encourage cutting corners unreasonably. The intended message is that auditors are usually experienced and reasonable people, but they are auditing against the ISO 9000 standards — not against what is reasonable — and should not be asked to take the responsibility to exempt the auditee from a clearly stated requirement.

When and where to perform the inspection

Receiving inspection does not always need to be carried out at the point of receiving. ISO 9000 Section 4.10.2.1 states that the product must be verified before it is used or processed. A system where materials and components are inspected on the production floor just prior to being used in production is technically acceptable. The inspection must still be an independent operation preceding any production process. It is not acceptable that process operators inspect the materials or components issued to them for processing. If the inspection is carried out directly in the production areas, the inspection stations must be separated, or other effective measures must be employed to prevent uninspected or nonconforming products from being used in production.

Best to verify/inspect upon receipt

Usually there is nothing to gain from postponing the receiving inspection until materials or components are issued for production. The same formal inspection system must be applied and, in addition, special arrangements are required in storage and production to separate the uninspected materials. Receiving inspection should be carried out at the point of receiving, unless there are special reasons to do otherwise.

Supplier vs subcontractor = standard vs custom products

There is a direct relationship between the controls employed for qualification and monitoring of vendors and the methods and scope employed in receiving inspection. These activities complement each other and have a common purpose — to ensure the quality of purchased products. The responsibilities, depth of scope, and product classifications adopted for the qualification of suppliers and subcontractors should be paralleled in the receiving inspection system. Many underlying concepts and considerations applicable to receiving inspection are the same as those applicable to purchasing. They are explained in Chapter 7, Purchasing Department, and will not be repeated in this section, except for the short summary that follows.

The distinction between suppliers and subcontractors was introduced in Chapter 7. Suppliers were defined to be those vendors that supply noncritical standard catalog products, and subcontractors to be vendors supplying products that are either modified or designed to satisfy special requirements, or are intended for critical applications. This distinction forms the basis for the dual track vendor evaluation system. The same considerations apply to receiving inspection.

Apply same distinction to receiving inspection

The receiving inspection system described below is based on the same distinction between suppliers and subcontractors. The distinction is relevant in most cases, but even when it is not, companies can pick those elements of the system that are applicable to their situation, regardless of how they differentiate between different classes of vendors and whether they do at all.

Receiving clerk performs first-stage inspection

In this model, all received products pass through the first-stage inspection carried out by the receiving clerk, and the critical and custom products are, in addition, subjected to the second-stage technical inspection carried out by the quality control inspectors.

Verify shipment and documents, and visually inspect product

First, for all received products, the purchase order is pulled out, the shipment is verified for completeness, including any quality certificates or records that may have been requested, and the products are inspected visually (this process for the first-stage receiving inspection is described in detail in Chapter 8). If the products are standard catalog products, the inspection ends here. The purchase order is signed off and the products are stamped with the PASSED inspection stamp.

Segregate product for second-stage inspection

Products designated for further quality control inspection are moved to a dedicated inspection area. If there is no such dedicated area and the same receiving area is used for the second-stage inspections, the products must be clearly labeled with a warning that they have not yet been accepted. Clear identification of the inspection status of products held in the receiving and inspection areas is critical because, inevitably, products with different inspection status are moved around and inter-mingled during inspections.

Scope of receiving inspection depends on subcontractor's final inspection

The nature and scope of inspection and testing required for every type of product must be determined. In the words of ISO 9000 Section 10.2.2, "in determining the amount and nature of receiving inspection, consideration shall be given to the controls exercised by the subcontractor". In practice, it means that the amount and scope of receiving inspection can be reduced when the subcontractor has a formal final inspection system; the scope and reliability of their system is known; and there are records of their final inspection.

Can products be exempted from receiving inspection?

This is understandable, but what is the limit of this interpretation. The question very often asked is, "Does it mean that a company can completely exempt products from receiving inspection when it has full confidence in, and records from, the subcontractor's final inspection?" In my opinion the answer is "Yes, but . . ." The "but" is the scope of the subcontractor initial qualification and the means employed to monitor quality performance. Confidence must be based on evidence.

Evidence required for exemption from receiving inspection

How much and what kind of evidence an auditor would need to accept an exemption of a subcontractor's products from the receiving inspection depends on the specific circumstances. The reasonable minimum seems to be a copy of the subcontractor's quality manual; copies of relevant inspection procedures; and inspection reports, or at least a certificate of compliance, delivered with every shipment. Many auditors would add that the subcontractor's quality system should also be audited regularly if it is not certified.

Can testing certificates substitute receiving inspection?

A precedence supporting this liberal interpretation is the established practice of accepting steel testing certificates. Visual inspection of steel products is meaningless. What matters are the testing certificates delivered with the steel. These certificates are always accepted, even though customers normally do not audit steel mills (except for large and critical projects). There is no reason why inspection and testing certificates delivered by other kinds of subcontractors should not be recognized with a similar degree of confidence.

All products go through at least first-stage inspection upon receipt

In the last couple of paragraphs I used the phrase "exempted from receiving inspection", but it is best not to say these words during the certification audit. The auditors should be assured that all products are inspected, but in some cases the scope of the inspection comprises only verification of the test reports and certificates delivered with the products. Apart from the physical inspection itself, all the other elements of an inspection process are still present. The inspection record is still established and the products or their packaging are still labeled with the PASSED inspection status identification.

The arcane interpretations discussed above are only relevant in special situations when a complete receiving inspection is not practical or would be a wasteful duplication of effort. However, in most companies there should be no need for elaborate interpretations. The received products should be simply inspected and tested.

Inspectors carrying out the receiving inspections should be equipped with copies of relevant purchase orders or contracts, as well as the drawings and specifications defining the received products. They should also use relevant inspection procedures and acceptance criteria

Ensure drawing revision level is documented in P.O. and that it is current

The drawings and specifications used by inspectors must be on the same revision level as those documents from which the products were manufactured. To audit compliance with this requirement is a simple matter. The revision levels of applicable drawings are normally specified on the purchase orders (and if they are not, this is in itself a noncompliance). The most vulnerable are those quality control departments that maintain their own drawing files. Auditors will be certain to check how those files are controlled. There must be a system assuring that new revisions of drawings are automatically distributed to these files and that obsolete drawings are removed and destroyed. If old revisions of drawings are used for inspection of spare parts for discontinued products, they can be kept in quality assurance but should be placed in separate files.

Inspectors should avoid making handwritten notes on drawings

Drawings used by inspectors are often marked with handwritten notes, comments and even changes. Making unauthorized changes is an indisputable noncompliance. But even notes and comments can lead to trouble. If these notes and comments are additional instructions necessary to carrying out inspections, they ought to be authorized and officially issued, preferably as separate work instructions. If they are only marked on a drawing, they will be lost when a new revision of the drawing is issued; or, to preserve their notes, inspectors will use both the old and the new drawing, which is completely unacceptable. For these reasons, drawings in the quality assurance department should be free of any handwritten notes or changes.

Establish written inspection procedures

The need for inspection procedures (instructions) for receiving inspection should be evaluated using the same considerations that generally apply to work instructions, as discussed in Chapter 10, Production Departments. My interpretation of the requirements for inspection instructions is rather liberal. But there are also auditors who believe there should be an inspection procedure for each kind of inspection. The arguments are that the aspects to examine, the techniques to use, the depth of the inspection, and the requirements for the format and contents of the inspection report and record are never obvious. It is hard to refute these arguments. To avoid any problems, I therefore also recommend that there be procedures for all types of inspections, without exception.

Form = document ....

The best format for inspection procedures are checklists or forms listing all inspection steps. When the actual values of the measured parameters must be recorded, forms have the advantage of providing both the listing of parameters that must be inspected and the fields for

Recorded results = record

recording the actual measurements. A form used in this way is first a document (a work instruction) and then, when the inspection is completed, it becomes a record of the inspection. Approving, issuing, and distributing this type of form must satisfy the requirements applicable to controlled documents.

Stipulate parameters that determine acceptance

Clear stipulation of the acceptance criteria for all types of inspections is an obvious, but surprisingly often violated, requirement. When the measured or tested parameters can be expressed in numerical values, the minimum and/or maximum acceptable values should be documented in a procedure, specification, or drawing. When the inspected aspects include appearance, color, faults, or surface finish, inspectors should be provided with descriptive specifications, photographs, or samples.

Document the receiving inspection system

In addition to the specific inspection instructions, the receiving inspection system should be documented in the quality manual and an operational procedure. The quality manual should explain the general functions of the receiving inspection system, and the operational procedure should instruct how to route different classes of products through the system and describe the principal steps for each stage of the receiving inspection.

IN-PROCESS INSPECTION

Inspect according to quality plan and hold until completed

Requirements pertaining to in-process inspections are stated in ISO 9000 Section 4.10.3, In-process inspection and testing. There are two requirements:

- That products shall be inspected and tested in accordance with the quality plan and/or documented procedures; and

- That products shall be held until the specified inspections and tests have been completed.

In-process inspections are not mandatory. If the quality plan does not prescribe any intermediate inspections, none need be carried out and the ISO 9000 standard is not violated.

Companies determine appropriate inspection requirements

Companies can determine for themselves how many and what kind of in-process inspections are appropriate for their particular products. Auditors normally do not challenge these decisions unless there is no inspection following a process whose results cannot be inspected later because they will be covered up by subsequent processing. In-process inspections are expected at the completion of such processes, although even in this case there is an alternative option. The process can be classified as a special process (i.e., the result of which cannot be verified by subsequent inspection) and the quality control effort can be shifted from inspection to process qualification and monitoring (see Chapter 10).

Are self-inspections part of the quality plan?

Some companies conduct in-process inspections but do not want to formalize them in their quality system. These are usually self-inspections carried out by production personnel upon completion of their operations. The philosophy is that the official inspections are conducted only by the quality control department, while the production department runs its own independent and unofficial inspection system to improve the efficiency of production and to screen the products before they reach the official inspection point.

Involvement of production personnel in a product verification system is a viable and positive contribution to the overall quality effort. However, it is unacceptable that in-process inspections be excluded from the quality system only because they are controlled by production rather than quality assurance.

Uncontrolled self-inspections jeopardize the quality system

Unofficial inspections violate the whole purpose of the quality system. If they are not documented in the quality plan, the consistency in their scope and application cannot be assured or verified. If the operators are not trained or equipped with inspection procedures, and do not use controlled measuring equipment, the results of the inspections may not be reliable. If the results of the inspections are not recorded, important information and data on process quality performance is lost. If the rejected products are not clearly labeled and segregated, there is the risk of them being used in production. There are so many potential violations associated with unofficial in-process inspections that they can be the sole reason for failing the certification audit.

Controlled self-inspections are a valid contribution to the inspection requirements

Bringing the production-controlled self-inspections into the quality system does not mean that the quality control department has to take over. The organization and responsibilities do not need to change, but the self-inspections must comply with the requirements applicable to all other inspections, and they must be specified in the quality plan. The production personnel must be trained and/or instructed by written procedures in the inspection techniques and acceptance criteria, and be equipped with controlled measuring equipment. The results of the inspections must be recorded, and there must be a system for handling nonconforming products.

In-process inspection is an element of final inspection

The need to formalize the in-process inspections ties in with the concept that they are, in fact, elements of the final inspection. When products are completed, the aspects inspected during production do not need to be inspected again at the final inspection. The person responsible for the final inspection and release of the product must have full confidence in the effectiveness of the in-process inspections and must verify that they were carried out with satisfactory results. Only a formal system of in-process inspections can provide this confidence.

Hold products until inspection is completed

The requirement that products be held until specified inspections and tests have been completed is usually satisfied by clear inspection status identification and designation of suitable holding areas. Both issues are discussed in detail in other chapters. To summarize the principles: All inspections must result in clear identification of the inspected products with their inspection status by stamping, marking or labeling the products, or signing off the accompanying work order. Products awaiting inspection or the next processing stage must be held in areas designated for this purpose.

FINAL INSPECTION

Scope of final inspection depends on product type

The principles on which the final inspection system should be based are identical to those that apply to the receiving and in-process inspections. All inspections must be called out by the quality plan; their scope and acceptance criteria must be defined; the inspectors must be trained and/or instructed by written procedures; only controlled measuring equipment can be used; the inspections must be recorded; and products must be identified with their inspection status. These issues have been or will be discussed in other sections of this chapter. This section will focus only on the special aspects of the final inspection; in particular verification of the quality records and the authorization to release product for shipping.

...And on inspection already performed

ISO 9000 Section 4.10.4, Final inspection and testing, explains the purpose of the final inspection: "... to complete the evidence of conformance of the finished product to the specified requirements." The phrasing of this statement suggests that the scope of the final inspection depends on how much inspection was done at receiving and during production. Only intermediate inspections that are documented and recorded, and that satisfy ISO 9000 requirements in all other respects, can be taken into account.

Provide final inspection checklist

Final inspection usually has a much broader scope than any of the intermediate inspections. Many different features of a product may need to be verified at this stage including, if applicable, functional and/or performance testing. In cases where it is not intuitively obvious what needs to be inspected, auditors will expect that inspectors are provided with checklists specifying the required inspections and tests.

Review all quality records for completeness

In addition to carrying out inspections and tests necessary to complete the evidence of conformance, the scope of the final inspection must include the review of all quality records that have been established during production. These records usually comprise sign-offs for completion of all specified processes and operations, sign-offs for intermediate inspections, and the traceability records. If all the records are contained on the work order accompanying a product or a batch of products, the task is straightforward; the work order is reviewed for completeness and correctness. Otherwise, all records need to be pulled together and verified.

Record final inspection results and identify products approved for shipping

After the specified inspections and testing are completed and the quality records are reviewed, the results of the final inspection must be recorded and the inspected products must be stamped, marked, or otherwise labeled to identify them as having passed the final inspection and being authorized for shipping. The inspection record can still be established by using the work order, but the identification of the inspection status and authorization to ship must be marked directly on the products or their packaging. At this stage the traveling work order is usually filed and will no longer be kept together with the products. The final inspection status identification must be especially clear and permanent as it also is an authorization to ship the products to customers.

Do not authorize product for shipping until all requirements are verified

In some companies the final inspection is carried out before completion of all operations, such as painting or installation of accessories. Strictly speaking, this is not the final inspection because at this stage the product does not conform to all specified requirements. If the nature of the production cycle or other circumstances require that the final inspection be carried out at that point, the scope and the procedure for this inspection does not need to be changed, but there should be one more inspection to verify the results of the remaining operations and processes. Which one of these inspections should be called the final inspection is a question of semantics and does not matter. What is important is that products not be authorized for shipping and not be identified as authorized before all specified requirements are verified.

The documentation of the general system for final inspections can have similar content and format as for other

**Document
final inspection
system**

types of inspections. But detailed procedures or check-lists stipulating the scope of final inspections are not optional, even in the simplest cases. Every inspection step must be documented for all types of products. There are two reasons why the scope of the final inspections must be documented. One is that there is usually a larger number of steps, including inspection and testing of numerous aspects of a product; verification that all operations and processes are completed; and review of previously established quality records. The second reason is that the customers may want to know what the scope is for final inspection so that they can adjust the scope of their receiving inspection accordingly.

INSPECTION STATUS IDENTIFICATION

There were two loopholes in the 1987 version of ISO 9000 that could be used to avoid implementation of the requirement for continuous maintenance of the inspection status identification during production. One was the allowance for the physical location of a product to be the identification of its inspection status, and the second was the words "as necessary", where it could be argued that inspection status identification was not necessary.

**Physical location
might not satisfy
identification
requirement**

In the 1994 revision of the standard, the option of physical location as the means for identifying inspection status is no longer mentioned explicitly. Instead, the standard calls for use of "suitable means" to identify the inspection status. Physical location can still be a suitable means but, not being mentioned directly, it is no longer accepted automatically. The auditee has to prove in each case that the physical location designated for holding or storage of products is sufficiently controlled to qualify as suitable means for the inspection status identification.

**No exceptions
to the status
identification
requirements**

The phrase "as necessary" has completely disappeared from the 1994 revision, closing the possibility for any exemptions. Accordingly, the current interpretation of ISO 9000 Section 4.12, Inspection and test status, is more stringent. For all practical purposes, the inspection status identification must be maintained continuously throughout all storage and production phases for all materials, components, and products, without exceptions.

Do purchased products require status identification?

The need to identify the inspection status of purchased products that passed receiving inspection is often disputed. When the storage areas are dedicated to only hold accepted materials and components, and there are records of receiving inspections, stamping every product with an inspection stamp seems to be superfluous. While I agree with this point of view, I hesitate to generally recommend that the physical location of the products in the storage and production areas be the only indication of their inspection status. Most companies do not have the kind of dedicated and secured storage areas and product receipt controls that would preclude an uninspected product entering these areas. But if indeed there are effective arrangements and administrative controls in this regard, the physical location of purchased products in the storage and production areas can be accepted as valid means for identifying their inspection status.

Identification by location will be scrutinized by auditors

An inspection status identification system based on physical location will be carefully evaluated by auditors. They will be looking for a clear policy authorizing such a system; procedures describing the measures employed to prevent entry of uninspected products to the controlled areas; convincing physical arrangements segregating these areas; and consistent implementation and maintenance of the system. Auditors will not accept the system if they see that some products are stamped with inspection stamps while others are not, and the discrimination is dictated by convenience rather than a coherent policy.

Work order can be used to identify status

Inspection status identification of products that move through the production cycle can be accomplished by using the work order. When the work order closely accompanies the products or is kept in the same area and can be quickly retrieved, the inspection sign-offs for in-process inspections called out on the work order provide the identification of the products' inspection status. A sign-off means that the inspection was carried out with a satisfactory result and an empty field means that the products are on hold awaiting inspection. A failed inspection can be identified by other means, such as a red tag or a label.

Or use stamps, tags or labels

When work orders are not used or cannot be adapted to this function, the most common method for identifying the inspection status is stamping, tagging, or labeling the products or the containers holding them. Physical location as inspection status identification can be justified in practice only on automated production lines. The machines or people doing the in-process inspections usually sort out and remove nonconforming products from the production line and, by the nature of the arrangement, only inspected and conforming products move on to the next processing stage. Even though this is clear and obvious, the decision to identify inspection status of products by their physical location on the production line must be documented in the quality manual or appropriate procedures to indicate that this is the official policy.

Most importantly, identify finished product

Proper and clear inspection status identification of finished products is the most important element of the inspection status identification system. The primary role of the status identification is to prevent uninspected and/or nonconforming products from being shipped to customers. The presence of a mark indicating that products passed the final inspection authorizes the shipping department to package and dispatch the products. The secondary role of marking products with the evidence that they passed the final inspection is to inform the customers that products were inspected before shipping. This information will help the customers adjust their receiving inspection scope and methods accordingly.

Products that are difficult to identify

The requirement for maintaining the inspection status identification throughout all stages of production and storage makes sense and is relatively easy to implement in most companies. However, there are situations when the effort to comply is significant but the benefits are not obvious. One of them is when a portion of material in bulk or liquid, or a couple of small components held in large batches, are taken out of storage. To maintain the inspection status identification, transfer containers would have to be stamped or labeled again to indicate that the products they contain have passed receiving inspection.

Where identification by location may be the solution

Practical solutions for a similar problem were suggested in Chapter 10 in the sections dealing with product identification and traceability. The same solutions can be adopted for the maintenance of inspection status identification. This may be going too far, however, especially when only standard noncritical materials and components are involved. In this situation, identification of the inspection status by physical location makes a lot of sense. Dedication of storage areas to contain only verified products and establishment of controls to prevent products from entering into production areas by another way may be a more effective and economical solution.

CONTROL OF NONCONFORMING PRODUCT

Nonconformity of product and noncompliance of quality system

Most people use the words *nonconformity* and *noncompliance* interchangeably, or use only one of these words to denote a product or a practice that does not fulfill or follow specified requirements. I use them both, and differentiate between their meaning. *Nonconformity*, as used in this book, is the nonfulfillment of one or more requirements specified for a product or service. *Noncompliance* is the nonfulfillment of quality system requirements specified in the ISO 9000 standard or in the quality system documentation. These are not official definitions, but such distinction promotes better communication when discussing quality systems.

Requirements for nonconforming product

The requirements pertaining to nonconforming products are contained in ISO 9000 Section 4.12, Inspection and test status, and in Section 4.13, Control of nonconforming product. The requirements are:

- Identification and segregation (when practical) of nonconforming products to prevent them from unintended use or dispatch;

- Documentation of the nature of nonconformity;
- Review and evaluation of nonconforming products;
- Determination of the disposition of the nonconforming products (accept, rework, regrade, or scrap); and
- Notification of other functions and/or departments affected by the nonconforming product.

Identify nonconforming product

The most common way to satisfy the requirement for identification of nonconforming products is marking, tagging, or labeling the products or their containers with clearly visible HOLD, NONCONFORMITY, or REJECTED labels. The background or the letters of these labels are usually red. The tags and labels must be firmly attached to the products. One detached tag usually does not provoke a noncompliance. But if auditors already have the perception that the method of attaching tags is ineffective and that nobody really cares if the tags are there or not, even one detached tag can become an issue.

Segregate nonconforming product

In addition to labeling, the nonconforming products should be segregated or even quarantined. Section 4.13.1 states that segregation is only required when practical. It means that large and heavy objects, large quantities of material in bulk or liquid, and other products that cannot be easily moved, can be exempted from the requirement for segregation. Auditors will not accept practices where the decision to segregate or not is based on what is convenient rather than what is practically possible and reasonable.

Varying degrees of segregation for different product

Different methods and degrees of segregation are expected for different kinds of nonconforming products. Small items are sufficiently segregated when they are held in a dedicated and clearly labeled box or bin. Large items that are not held in containers should be removed from the production flow. Purchased materials and components should be held in a quarantine or a designated section of the receiving area. Finished products should be also quarantined or held in a designated area away from products that are authorized for shipping. A good test to decide if the segregation is sufficient is to ask

"Would it be possible to confuse the nonconforming product with other products if the label identifying its nonconforming status was removed?" The answer must of course be "No."

Control quarantine areas

Quarantines are usually completely enclosed areas secured with a door or a gate that can be locked. Chain-link fences are often used for building quarantines. While fully enclosed and secured areas are mandatory in companies manufacturing regulated products, any area can be designated as a quarantine for non-critical products as long as it is sufficiently segregated and isolated. A rack of shelves or a cabinet identified with a QUARANTINE sign is an acceptable quarantine area.

Document, evaluate and disposition nonconformity

The second, third, and fourth requirement of Section 4.13 — documentation of the identified nonconformity, and evaluation and disposition of the nonconforming product — can be satisfied using a nonconformity report form. An example of this form is provided in the *ISO 9000 Documentation* reference book. The form has the following four sections:

- **Heading:** the rejected products are identified by name, part number, serial numbers, sales or purchase order numbers, and the vendor or department who manufactured them.

- **Description of nonconformity:** The nonconformity is described and the person who detected it is identified by title and signature.

- **Disposition:** Four disposition possibilities are listed: use-as-is, regrade, rework, and scrap. There is also space for comments and the required authorizing signatures. (Distinction between *rework* and *repair* should be made when relevant.)

- **Close-out:** Spaces are provided for referencing documents established in the course of correcting the nonconformity (corrective action requests and re-inspection reports) and for signatures evidencing that all actions required to close out the nonconformity report have been completed satisfactorily.

Anyone in company can initiate a nonconformity report

The first and second section of this form is filled out by the person who identified the nonconformity. Usually, it would be the quality control inspectors and production personnel responsible for inspection and testing of products, but nobody should be excluded. All other personnel should be encouraged to watch for and report nonconformities. The person initiating the nonconformity report should identify himself or herself by title and signature.

Determine disposition of nonconforming product

The next step is the disposition decision. Assignment of the responsibility for making this decision is an important issue. A nonconformity may be an isolated minor defect that can be reworked immediately without affecting quality or even appearance of the product or, to the other extreme, it may be a serious public safety hazard potentially involving a large number of products already shipped. To deal efficiently with such a broad spectrum of cases, it is useful to divide the possible nonconformities into a number of classes and assign to them different levels of authority for dispositions.

When it is obvious that the nonconforming product must be scrapped or regraded, or it can be reworked without affecting its quality, the disposition decision can be left with the quality control inspector who identified the problem and/or the foreman who is responsible for the operation or process that caused it. In cases when an use-as-is disposition is a possibility, a repair would degrade quality, or a large number of products are affected, the disposition decision should be made on a higher level and may require the involvement of several departments.

Re-inspect reworked product

The last section on the nonconformity report form is used for closing out the report. Use-as-is, regrade, and scrap decisions do not require any further actions and the report can be closed out immediately by the same person who made the disposition decision. But the rework (and repair) decisions must be followed up with re-inspection. In this case the nonconformity report is closed out by the inspector who verified that the reworked products fully conform with specified requirements.

Notify depart-ments affected by nonconform-ing product

The last requirement of ISO 9000 Section 4.13 is notification of other functions and/or departments affected by the nonconforming product. This can be done by distributing the nonconformity report to the interested parties. When the nonconforming product is delivered by a vendor, the purchasing department should be notified. When it is a product that is returned by a customer, the sales and customer service departments should receive copies of the report. When the delivery schedule is impacted by the identified nonconformity, the contract administration function must be informed. Quality assurance should have copies of all nonconformity reports to analyze trends and make decisions on preventive and corrective actions that may be required.

Some companies also identify causes of nonconformities

The above-described procedure for dealing with nonconforming products is the minimum acceptable system that satisfies the requirements of ISO 9000. But many companies go further. In addition to documenting and evaluating nonconforming products, they collect data needed to investigate and correct the causes of nonconformities. The relevant information is precise identification of the operation or process responsible for the nonconformity and identification of the possible causes. Examples of typical causes include use of nonconforming materials, use of defective or inappropriate tools, wrong machine setting or process parameters, operator error, inadequate operator qualifications, or faulty design or specification. Classification and documentation of causes is invaluable for tracking trends and planning preventive actions.

Does every nonconforming product need to be documented?

The question that is often asked is, "Do we need to document and report every single nonconforming product?" Companies manufacturing individual custom products or small series of relatively complex products would normally need to report every single occurrence of nonconforming material, component, and product. But in mass production manufacturing where certain levels of rejects are expected, only excessive levels of a specific nonconformity need to be documented.

150 ISO 9000 QUALITY SYSTEM

Mandatory if product-related condition is not normal

Many companies do not report nonconformities that are "trivial". If the nonconformity can be corrected or the product can be scrapped before it reaches the next inspection point, they do not see the need for documenting the nonconformity. This is a symptom of an unofficial inspection program existing outside the formal quality system. This situation was discussed in the section dealing with in-process inspections, and why such practices are unacceptable was explained.

Every nonconformity, no matter how trivial it is, has its causes. If it is not documented, the causes may never be identified and corrected. One of the major objectives of a quality system is continuous improvement. This cannot be achieved if the level of rejects for each operation and the associated causes are not known.

MEASURING AND TEST EQUIPMENT

The most detailed and specific requirements in the ISO 9000 standard

ISO 9000 Section 4.11, Control of inspection, measuring, and test equipment, is by far the most detailed and specific section in the whole standard. It is so strikingly different in its approach that it makes the other sections look like mere outlines. I always wondered what was so special about measuring equipment that it deserved throwing the ISO 9000 standard out of balance by introducing such inconsistency in the approach. Measuring equipment is important because it is used to verify conformity with specified requirements. But the other elements of a quality system are equally as important.

The advantage of the requirements being stated in such specific manner is that there is no need to interpret or second guess the requirements. Documentation and implementation of the requirements is just a matter of starting with point a) and finishing on point i). The disadvantage is that the same is true for auditing the compliance. It is the easiest area to audit. Auditor trainees are usually first assigned to audit the calibration functions before they are allowed to audit any other department.

ISO 9000 requires that only measuring and testing equipment used for verification of products must be calibrated. It allows the equipment used in production and maintenance of machines to be excluded from the control system.

Equipment used in production optional but recommended

I never liked this differentiation between equipment used in production and that used in inspection. It prevents the production personnel from contributing to the product verification effort and it invalidates process monitoring and control. When I audit a company where only quality control inspectors use calibrated equipment, I immediately develop the feeling that the name of the game is not implementing a modern quality system, but simply getting the ISO 9000 certificate. If the additional cost of controlling production measuring equipment is not excessive, I would recommend that all measuring equipment be calibrated. This will also save the cost and effort of separating equipment with different calibration status.

Identify uncontrolled measuring equipment

Measuring equipment that is not controlled must be labeled with a warning that it is not calibrated and a procedure must instruct that such equipment may not be used for inspections and testing. Uncontrolled equipment should be stored separately. Equipment that is damaged or is not maintained must be also labeled and separated or, even better, quarantined in a locked cabinet.

Measuring equipment is either controlled or not controlled

Labeling measuring equipment with FOR REFERENCE ONLY stickers does not make any sense unless the required accuracy and limitations of use are defined. If there is a real need for reference measurements where high accuracy is not required, the REFERENCE ONLY equipment can be checked using other formally calibrated equipment instead of using calibration standards. But the resulting loss of accuracy must be calculated and documented. From the perspective of ISO 9000, the measuring and testing equipment is either controlled or is not controlled. There are no alternatives.

The backbone of any calibration control system is a list of all controlled measuring and testing equipment. Every

Maintain list for all controlled measuring and test equipment

piece of equipment on the list is identified by its type and serial number, its usual location, the prescribed calibration periodicity, the last calibration date, and the next due date for calibration. The list is usually maintained on a computer. A standard database or a specialized program for management of measuring equipment can be used for this purpose.

Identify measuring equipment with calibration stickers

All controlled measuring equipment must be marked with calibration stickers and the calibration must be evidenced with a certificate. As a minimum, the calibration certificate should precisely identify the piece of equipment, the standard that was used for calibration and its traceability number to the corresponding national standard, and the calibration date. When relevant, the certificate should also indicate the ambient temperature during calibration and the accuracy of the equipment. Certificates for comparative reference hardware, such as blocks, rings, gauges, or jigs, should provide the actual dimensions as measured.

Document work instructions

The last principal element of a calibration system is work instructions for calibrating various types of measuring equipment. I personally do not believe that calibrating is different from any other process and would advocate that work instructions are only necessary when special skills, beyond those that can be learned from a simple demonstration, are required. However, I am often at odds with my colleagues on this issue. Most auditors expect to see work instructions for all types of measuring equipment calibrated in-house, without any exceptions.

Other requirements

These three elements — equipment list, calibration certificates and stickers, and work instructions — are the pillars of the calibration control system. Any serious problem with any one of them means a failed audit. But there are also other requirements:

- Accuracy of measuring equipment must be known and documented. If equipment manuals do not specify the accuracy capability, it should be checked and recorded on the calibration certificate.

- When appropriate, environmental conditions (usually temperature or pressure) must be controlled during calibration. The instrument measuring the controlled parameter must also be calibrated and the level of the parameter must be recorded on the calibration certificate.

- The measuring equipment must be safeguarded from unauthorized adjustments that would invalidate the calibration setting. The most effective measure is to seal the adjustments screws, but this is not always possible. It is generally sufficient to state in a procedure and/or a warning label that unauthorized adjustments are prohibited.

- The measuring equipment must be adequately preserved, stored, and handled. Auditors take this requirement seriously. Measuring equipment stored without protective boxes or intermingled with tools and other unrelated items often provokes a noncompliance.

- Validity of measurements made with equipment that is found to be out of calibration must be formally assessed. To demonstrate compliance, a procedure should prescribe a course of action for this situation. Formal corrective action requests are usually issued to trace back and identify the affected products.

- Test software must be included in the control system. It must be formally validated and authorized before it is installed, and be otherwise controlled just like any other kind of testing equipment.

Minor vs major noncompliances

The majority of noncompliances found by auditors during certification audits pertain to individual pieces of equipment. It can be a misplaced calibration certificate, a lost calibration sticker, a piece of equipment that cannot be located, and so forth. As long as there are not too many of them, these are minor noncompliances and will not weigh heavily on the final verdict. The more serious noncompliances are when an element of a system is missing or is not adequately documented or implemented (for example, the accuracy of equipment is generally not known, environmental conditions are not taken into account, test gauges and jigs are not checked regularly, the equipment is not adequately protected, and so forth).

12 PACKAGING AND SHIPPING

ISO 9000 requirements relevant to the shipping department are stated primarily in ISO 9000 Section 4.15.4, Packaging, and in Section 4.15.6, Delivery. Both sections are very short and general. Packaging is relevant in almost all companies. Delivery is only relevant when shipping is included in the contract, and especially when the company maintains its own transportation equipment.

Packaging requirements are simple to understand and implement, but often are not adequately addressed. Packaging is very important in preserving the quality of products and it is natural that the quality system should be concerned with its control. But in practice, quality assurance often stops at the final inspection and does not extend to comprise the packaging and shipping activities. An ISO 9000 quality system should be concerned with the quality of products as they are received by the the customer. When products are damaged during storage and/or transportation, the customer will not benefit from the quality that was built into them during design and production.

PACKAGING

Product packaging vs shipping packaging

There are usually two levels of packaging for most kinds of products. The packaging that directly contains the product, is referred to as *product packaging,* and the packaging that protects products during delivery is called *shipping packaging.* In most companies product packaging and shipping packaging are two completely different operations.

Product packaging is usually the last production operation, preceded by final inspection and followed by placement of finished products in storage. The shipping packaging is usually done just prior to the dispatch of an order and is carried out in the shipping area. ISO 9000 does not differentiate between product and shipping packaging. The same text of the standard applies, but the interpretation must differ. While product packaging is often specific to a product and may play an important function in connection with the use of the product, the shipping packaging has the sole purpose of protecting products during delivery and storage, and is adapted to the means of handling and transportation rather than the products it contains.

Specify and approve packaging and marking

Section 4.15.4 states that packing, packaging, and marking processes shall be controlled to ensure conformance to specified requirements. Although the statement seems rather vague, it contains two important requirements. The first is that packaging and marking must be specified and approved. The second is that the operations of packaging and marking must be controlled with reference to the same criteria that apply to production processes and operations.

Control the design of the product package

Product packaging is a part of the total product offering. The same requirements that apply to design of products are also applicable to design of product packaging. When standard boxes or bags are used, it is sufficient that the packaging is defined in drawings, specifications, or procedures, and that it is approved. The design process and/or the criteria for choosing the packaging will not be scrutinized. However, when the packaging must meet certain performance requirements, auditors will expect that the packaging design process is documented and includes clear identification of the design input criteria and verification of the packaging. Typical examples of engineered packaging are containers holding liquids, cans, vacuum bags, sterile packaging, and boxes and crates that must withstand specified stacking or impact loads.

Requirements for packaging processes similar to production

The material used for product packaging should be formally specified and be purchased from approved suppliers or subcontractors. It must be subjected to the receiving inspection just as all other materials used for manufacturing of products. Also, the packaging processes must satisfy the same criteria as those discussed in Chapter 10 for production processes. The need for work instructions, personnel training, process procedures, process monitoring, and control of the environment must be evaluated using these criteria.

Packaging requirements must be documented

Shipping packaging is normally not considered to be a part of the product offering, unless it has other functions in addition to protecting products during delivery and storage. Accordingly, purchasing control and receiving inspections are usually not required for such standard packaging materials as cardboard boxes, crates, or pallets. But regardless of how standardized it is, all shipping packaging must be defined in drawings, specifications, or procedures. If there are particular performance criteria specified for the shipping packaging, auditors may ask for evidence that these criteria are satisfied.

Control printed information or packaging artwork

Section 4.15.4 explicitly requires that marking of packaging must be controlled. It is not clear if the requirement applies to all artwork printed on product packaging or only to the shipping marking, or both. There is no universal agreement among auditors on the interpretation, but it does not make any difference. Even if this section is applied only to shipping marking, the product packaging artwork must still be controlled because it is a part of the total product offering.

Product packaging often displays instructions and notices that are important to the effective and safe use of the product. These can be product specifications, operating instructions, and warning notices. Therefore, the printed information must be reviewed, authorized, and documented in a formal way. Either Section 4.15.4, Packaging, or Section 4.9, Process control, can be used as the basis for this requirement.

The best way to control the artwork of product packaging is to issue it as a drawing, and apply the same review, approval, and revision controls as are applied to drawings defining products. The shipping packaging marking is best controlled by procedures or work instructions specifying what marking should be applied for different kinds of shipments, for example export, domestic, air, ground, or sea.

Properly document and communicate customer requirements

The system for controlling shipping packaging and marking must also provide for communication and implementation of special customer and/or shipper requirements. Auditors often ask how such requirements are transmitted to the shipping department. Instructions scribbled on margins of shipping orders or on self-stick notes will not be accepted. The shipping order forms should have designated fields for documenting special packaging and marking instructions. Shippers usually document their requirements in their manuals or standards. These should be available in the shipping department.

Provide formal specifications for packaging and marking

The most serious, but surprisingly common, noncompliance in the shipping department is the complete lack of formal specifications for packaging and marking. Normally it would mean a failed audit, but it is so common that, if everything else is in order, auditors often downgrade the importance of this noncompliance to avoid failing practically every other company they audit. The vague and convoluted language in Section 4.15.4 is partly responsible for this problem.

DELIVERY

Requirements apply only when delivery is specified by contract

The requirements stated in ISO 9000 Section 4.15.6, Delivery, are only applicable where the delivery of products to customers, or intermediate locations such as a shippers warehouse, is specified in the contract. Those companies that never ship or are not responsible for shipping their products need only state so in their quality manual and pledge that in the event shipping is specified in any future contract, the protection of products will be extended to include delivery to destination.

Control the selection and monitoring of the shipper

Those companies that are responsible for shipping their products, but do not transport the products themselves, must demonstrate that appropriate controls are exercised in the selection and monitoring of the shippers subcontracted to deliver products. In other words, shippers must be controlled like any other supplier or subcontractor. They should be evaluated, their quality performance should be monitored, and they should be included in the approved supplier/subcontractor list.

Requirements for companies that deliver their own product

The most exposed are the companies that provide their own delivery service. To what extent the delivery operations must comply with all the 20 sections of ISO 9000 is not clearly stated and the interpretation is not agreed upon. The most stringent interpretation is that delivery is a part of the total product offering and thus all activities related to delivery must be audited against the whole standard, as if delivery operation was an independent shipping company. On the other extreme, if Section 4.15.6 is taken literally, controls are expected only for the delivery operation activities directly related to the protection of products.

Application of the broad interpretation

If the broad interpretation is applied, there must be procedures regulating handling of delivery orders, management of delivery scheduling, loading and unloading of delivery vehicles, fastening of loads, maintenance of delivery vehicles, routing of delivery receipts, and so forth. Fortunately for the auditees most auditors do not interpret the standard in this way, and even if they would like to, there is not enough time during the audit to go into such details. But in companies where delivery of products is an important part of the operation — distributors, for example — auditors may very well decide to apply the whole standard against all activities related to delivery.

Requirements for the protection of product

The more common way to audit the delivery operations is to focus on those activities that directly pertain to product protection. The relevant issues are loading and unloading techniques, fastening of loads, protection of loads against adverse atmospheric conditions, and preservation of perishable goods.

In most cases the handling and protection of product is quite standard and even obvious. Products are stacked on pallets, forklift trucks are used for loading, the load is strapped or shimmed, and, if required, the load is protected against water damage with a tarpaulin.

Document standard handling and protection of product requirements

When such standard handling techniques are involved, it is sufficient to issue a general procedure that describes the handling activities, to include prescribing rules for stacking heights for crates or pallets, specifying techniques for fastening the loads, and defining the means to be used to protect products from rain and snow. It is important to include an element of inspection in the procedure. Drivers or other personnel could be instructed to check that the load is properly fastened and protected before leaving the loading dock.

Other product protection issues

If products can deteriorate over a short period of time or controlled environmental conditions are required during transportation, the procedure should also address these aspects.

Control design of engineered fastenings

In cases where the loading and/or fastening techniques and methods need to be engineered, the design must be documented and supported by calculations. Typical examples are the transportation of unusually heavy or bulky loads, or when heavy chains, bolting or welding are required for fastening the load. The engineering, manufacturing, and installation of such fastenings must comply with the same ISO 9000 requirements that apply to engineering and manufacturing of products.

13 SERVICE AND SERVICING

ISO 9000 Section 4.19, Servicing, is very peculiar. It consists of one 29-word sentence stating that the servicing functions and verification of servicing must be documented in procedures. The brevity of this section and the lack of specifics could suggest that ISO 9000 does not place much importance on servicing. But the title of the standard suggests just the opposite. Servicing is explicitly named in the title, indicating that every single requirement in the ISO 9000 standard must be applied to the servicing functions.

In this context it is understandable why Section 4.19 is so short and vague. If it named any specific requirements, it would suggest that only the named requirements apply to servicing. It should not be necessary to employ such arcane interpretations to understand the intent of the standard. Section 4.19 could either directly state that the whole standard applies, or it could be completely taken out, leaving it solely to the title to define the scope of application of the standard. This approach is used for installation. The installation functions are explicitly named in the title of the standard, but there is no section with separate requirements for installation.

Consult ISO 9004 for guidance in interpretation of standard

Interpretation of ISO 9000 for servicing, and especially for services, is not obvious. Some guidance is provided in ISO 9004 Part 1, Quality management and quality system elements — Guidelines, and in ISO 9004 Part 2, Quality management and quality system elements — Guidelines for services, which is especially relevant. ISO 9004 requirements are not mandatory for passing the ISO 9000 certification audit, but they should be con-

162 **ISO 9000 QUALITY SYSTEM**

sulted whenever an ISO 9000 requirement needs clarification or interpretation.

In manufacturing industries the following two types of activities fall under servicing:

- **Customer service:** Handles customer complaints and provides customers with product information regarding technical specifications, modes of use, operating instructions, interfacing with other products or systems, etc.

- **Product Servicing:** Provides maintenance and repair services, issues maintenance manuals, provides training to customers or servicing subcontractors, and coordinates production and distribution of spare parts. Product servicing also collects field experience and product reliability data.

Requirements for service providers are not discussed

Some companies sell services that are not directly related to any specific product (for example, training, consulting, or project management). The operation providing such services must also comply with the ISO 9000 standard unless they are not mentioned in the scope of the ISO 9000 certificate. As most manufacturing companies either do not provide independent services or elect not to include them in the scope of the certificate, the interpretation of ISO 9000 for service providers is not discussed in this chapter. It is a topic that merits a dedicated book, and until such a book is published, I recommend consulting ISO 9004 Part 2, Quality systems and quality system elements — Guidelines for services.

CUSTOMER SERVICE AND CUSTOMER COMPLAINTS

Assign the customer service function

Every company interacts and communicates with their customers after the sale. Customers may have questions regarding technical specifications of the products and interfacing with other products or equipment, and questions pertaining to installation, use, and maintenance of products. They may want to complain about the quality and performance of the products. In large companies there is usually a separate customer service department that deals with customer questions and complaints. In smaller companies the customer service function is often assigned to a unit within the marketing, sales, or engineering department. But there are also companies that do not have any formal system for handling customer questions and complaints.

Define who handles customer complaints

In preparation for the ISO 9000 certification, every company should review its organization charts and specifications of departmental responsibilities to assure that the customer service function is represented and defined. If the nature of the products is such that a full scope customer service function is not necessary, the organizational chart or at the least the specification of responsibilities should define who handles customer complaints.

"How are customer complaints recorded, routed and responded to?"

To ISO 9000 auditors, handling of customer complaints is the most important function of the customer service. Customer support and product support are not mentioned directly in the standard and auditors will not challenge (although they may wonder about) the nonexistence of these functions. However, a system for handling customer complaints is always expected, without exceptions. The question, "How are customer complaints recorded, routed, and responded to?" is on every auditor's checklist. If the system for handling customer complaints is not documented, there is a clear noncompliance. The ISO 9000 section invoked in this case is Section 4.14.2, Corrective action, where customer complaints are mentioned explicitly.

Document responsibility, communication and corrective action

The basic elements for handling customer complaints should be documented in a procedure, to include:

- appointment of a department or a person that is responsible for receiving customer complaints;
- the manner of recording and filing the complaints;
- communication with other departments and functions concerned;
- initiation of corrective actions; and
- communication with the customer.

Complaints need to be logged, recorded, organized, communicated and closed

The mail room, the fax room and the telephone switchboard operators should know where to direct customer complaints. All written complaints should be logged, and verbal complaints should be reported on special forms or in memos. Complaints that are being processed should be organized in files or ring binders so that the status of a complaint is easy to follow. Communication with other departments or functions should be recorded. There should be a clear policy for responding to the customer and for making decisions regarding refunds, exchanges, and repairs. The process and authorizations required for closing out a customer complaint should be defined, and the retention period for closed-out complaints should be specified.

Corrective action under separate procedure

Handling of corrective and preventive actions initiated by customer complaints is usually regulated by a separate system. The customer service department or function is seldom qualified to analyze the root causes of the underlying problems and make appropriate decisions. The system should stipulate that all customer complaints pertaining to quality of products or associated services be reported to the quality assurance department. The quality assurance department then analyzes the underlying problems, and determines if and what corrective actions are required. Initiating and processing corrective actions are discussed in Chapter 16.

Generally differentiate between customer complaints and corrective action procedures

ISO 9000 suggests that the system for handling customer complaints be described in procedures dealing with corrective action. This might be a good approach for small companies where the same department deals with both customer complaints and corrective actions. However, when different departments are responsible for these functions, it is best to issue two separate procedures. Also, the established auditing practice is to differentiate between customer complaints and corrective action. For larger audits the audit itineraries often list them as separate items.

PRODUCT SERVICING

When servicing
is not applicable
or is subcon-
tracted...

Not all companies manufacture serviceable products, and even those that do may not service the products themselves. When products are not serviceable, the quality manual should state that servicing of products is not applicable, and this is all that needs to be done. If servicing is subcontracted or licensed externally, auditors may want to see evidence that subcontractors are selected on the basis of their qualifications, and that support and training are provided when required.

When in
doubt, ask
your registrar

Auditors usually will not go into great depth to verify the controls applied to subcontracting and licensing of product servicing unless the products are machines or durable consumer goods such as industrial machines, office machines, computers, household appliances, or automobiles. If in doubt, I recommend that candidates for ISO 9000 certification ask their registrars what the requirements are in this regard.

Theoretical
vs practical

Companies that provide their own product servicing should, strictly speaking, document and implement all relevant requirements of the whole ISO 9000 standard in their servicing departments. Although in theory this is an undeniably true statement; in practice it may be an overstatement. I know from experience that many auditors will let servicing go with much less than compliance with the whole standard.

It depends on
where servicing
fits in the
company

When servicing is only a peripheral activity, auditors will not spend much time investigating this function. Many practices that would provoke a noncompliance in production may be accepted in servicing. But there is really no guaranteeing the outcome of the audit. It depends on the importance of servicing, on the history of quality problems in this area, and on the auditor and his or her impression of the servicing department and the whole company.

To avoid advising implementation of potentially unnecessary systems, I will limit the discussion that follows to only those elements of quality systems applicable to ser-

Elements where noncompliances most frequent

vicing where the most frequent noncompliances are found:

- Organization of work flow, segregation of products with different status, and containment of disassembled products;
- Control of spare parts;
- Documentation of scope of repairs and maintenance, and work instructions; and,
- Verification of servicing.

No matter how difficult, a quality system is required for servicing

Many companies that are otherwise reasonably close to achieving compliance with ISO 9000 have servicing departments that do not operate any kind of quality system. It is true that it is more difficult to implement quality systems in servicing than in production. In servicing, the scope of work is only known ahead of time for scheduled routine maintenance, but it cannot be predicted for the repair of malfunctioning products before they are diagnosed. It is also difficult to physically arrange the work flow of operations and processes for servicing because every product needs different processing, and it is not practical to move disassembled products around. Auditors are aware of these difficulties, but these problems cannot be the excuse for not having a quality system in servicing.

Service area must look like there is a quality system

The first impression is crucial. When auditors walk through the servicing area they must immediately see and feel that a quality system is present. In most companies the impression is just the opposite. The appearance of a servicing area that would disqualify it on the spot include boxes and shelves overflowing with semi-scrapped products and parts; inadequate containment and protection of disassembled customer products; lack of proper identification of products and parts; messy workbenches; uncontrolled and mistreated measuring and testing equipment; and so forth. When the servicing area is hardly distinguishable from a junk yard, auditors know that if a quality system in servicing exists at all, it can only be a hoax.

Organization of work flow and separation of different operations and processes is not as easy in servicing as it is in production. In servicing, products usually do not move from one operation to another, but are often permanently placed on a servicing bench and all operations are carried out on that bench. Such an environment is difficult to control, but it can be done.

Segregate certain operations and organize holding and storage areas

Operations that can contaminate and/or damage other products, such as cleaning, welding, and painting, should be segregated. Trays, bins, boxes, and other containers should be used to contain dismantled products to prevent intermingling of parts. When the servicing of products is on hold awaiting parts or customer decisions, the products should be removed from the servicing benches and placed in designated holding areas. Equipment, tools, supplies, and parts used in servicing should have designated storage locations and be kept there when not in use. Servicing benches should be cleared and cleaned after completion of every operation and process, and so forth.

Caution advised concerning semi-scrapped products

Most damaging is the presence of semi-scrapped products and parts in the servicing areas. This is a distinct indication that there is a practice of incorporating used parts in the serviced products. If the used parts are not reconditioned and/or inspected, and are not properly identified with a part number and inspection status, the noncompliance is so serious that the whole audit can be failed for this reason alone. As for new products, all parts used in servicing must be purchased from approved suppliers or be manufactured in-house under the same controls that apply to manufacturing new products. Also, they must be inspected and marked with inspection status identification, and they must be identified by a part number.

Segregate and identify serviced product

It is difficult to implement these requirements when spare parts are stored in the servicing area. They should either be stored with other new parts that are used in production, or the servicing area should have its own designated and segregated storage. Defective parts dismantled from the serviced products should be immediately placed in scrap containers or otherwise segregated. The same segregation requirement applies to products whose servicing has been abandoned because of excessive cost or unreasonableness of the required repairs.

Control reconditioned parts

Companies manufacturing specialized or custom machines with long life cycles often rely on the use of reconditioned parts in servicing. To assure supply of such parts, the broken up and scrapped machines are retained and dismantled when parts are needed. ISO 9000 does not object to such practices as long as they are officially sanctioned, documented, and controlled.

Quarantine, inspect, recondition, and identify used parts

The area where the scrapped machines are stored must be enclosed and secured like a quarantine. All the dismantled parts must be formally inspected against defined acceptance criteria and be reconditioned when required. The parts must be identified with a part number and a passed inspection status identification before they are stored in the servicing area or are incorporated into the serviced machines.

The service plan is equivalent to the production plan

Planning and documenting the operations and processes required to service a product is more difficult than planning for new production. It can be done ahead of time only for scheduled routine maintenance. The service plan for the repair of malfunctioning or damaged products cannot be established before the products are inspected, tested, and diagnosed. Although difficult, compliance with the requirement for planned servicing cannot be exempted.

How to "plan" servicing

A brief report with a description of the malfunctioning feature and a list of things to be done to correct the problem constitutes a sufficient servicing plan. The list can be issued in the form of a servicing order similar to the work order discussed in Chapter 6, Production Planning. Many companies do not formally plan and document all servicing operations before they are performed, but the details of the servicing are recorded after it is completed. Strictly speaking, this is not good enough.

However, if the record is established by identifying and recording each operation before it is started and signing off at completion, the illusion of planning ahead of time is sufficient for most auditors to accept the system. The bottom line is that some kind of paperwork identifying each servicing job should accompany the serviced products.

Evaluate need for work instructions

The evaluation of the need for work instructions in servicing can be based on exactly the same criteria that apply in production. Instructions are expected when the required level of skill exceeds what can be learned in the course of a simple on-the-job demonstration.

Train the technicians

An additional factor in servicing is the training of technicians. Inspecting, testing, and diagnosing malfunctioning products often requires considerable knowledge, experience, and skill. Auditors will expect that the qualification criteria for service technicians are defined and that specialized training is provided when required.

Final inspect/test servicing

The last issue in this section is verification of servicing. The considerations are similar to those related to servicing planning. Strictly speaking, there should be a documented quality plan for servicing just as there is for production. But while auditors will not accept serviced products being shipped to customers without any inspecting and/or testing, they usually do not insist on a detailed quality plan. It is normally sufficient when there is a record identifying the final inspections and tests that were performed, without them being formally planned ahead of time.

Document the quality system in servicing

Documentation of the quality system in servicing may need to be relatively extensive. Systems used in servicing are often quite different from those used in production which, to the extreme, may require different procedures for contracting and selling servicing, preparing servicing and quality plans, controlling spare parts, controlling servicing operations and processes, and verifying the servicing. However, in smaller companies and in companies where servicing is only a peripheral activity, it is normally sufficient to have one operational procedure explaining all aspects of servicing from contract review to verification.

Address servicing in other procedures

The elements of the quality system that are similar for servicing and new product manufacturing can be addressed by reference to other procedures, even if there are some differences. If, for example, the process for contracting servicing has some aspects that are different from the process for contracting new products, a subsection explaining the differences can be added to the general contract review procedure, thus avoiding the need to issue a separate procedure for contracting servicing.

FIELD EXPERIENCE AND RELIABILITY DATA

ISO 9000 does not directly require collecting and analyzing field experience and reliability data. Only section 4.14.3, Preventive action, mentions service reports as one of the sources of information that should be used to identify quality problems. But ISO 9004 is much more explicit in this regard. Section 16.5, Post marketing surveillance, directly encourages reporting instances of product failure and implementing appropriate corrective actions in design, processing, and/or use of the product.

Collect and communicate product performance and reliability data

Thus, the ISO 9000 standards provide auditors with a sufficient base to identify a noncompliance when there is no formal system obliging servicing to collect product performance and reliability data, and communicate it to quality assurance, design, and production departments. Regardless of how ISO 9000 addresses this issue, the failure to document and communicate the experiences in servicing is a serious shortcoming of a quality system. It impairs the system's ability to improve the quality of products. Auditors will be suspicious of a system that neglects such an invaluable source of information.

Report product failures

The simplest way to report occurrences of product failure is to collect and distribute the inspection, testing, and diagnostic reports that servicing establishes to determine the scope of required repairs. When appropriate, the failed parts can be also retained and analyzed. Another way is to oblige servicing to issue a periodical report summarizing the modes and reasons for product failure.

System for analyzing performance data

In addition to objective evidence for data being collected and communicated, auditors will also want to see the evidence that the data is analyzed and used. Auditors normally will not question the means and methods employed to collect and analyze the data. What they care about is that there is a system regulating these activities, that the system is documented in a procedure, and that it is implemented consistently.

14 TRAINING

Identification of
training needs

Definition of
training program

Qualification
of instructors

Maintenance of
training records

All ISO 9000 requirements pertaining to personnel training are stated in Section 4.18, Training. The section is rather short and general and, as often happens in this standard, there are no clearly identifiable specific requirements. There are, however, some clues contained in such phrases as *documented procedures, identifying training needs, providing training,* and *training records.* But fortunately, even though the standard is vague, the auditing practice in this area is well established, and auditors usually apply very similar criteria when judging the adequacy of the training system.

The basic elements that auditors expect to be documented and implemented in a training system are:

- Mechanisms for identification of training needs;
- Definition and documentation of the scope and form of training;
- Qualification of instructors; and
- Maintenance of training records.

TRAINING NEEDS

Personnel training can be divided into several broad categories:

- Companywide training of all personnel in such matters as general orientation about the company and its products, the functioning of the quality system, and safety in the workplace.

- Interdepartmental training offered to large groups of personnel, explaining the use of widely implemented equipment and systems, such as computers, databases, bar code systems, or part numbering and marking system.

- Departmental training provided to technical personnel, supervisors, and operators to teach or improve the knowledge and skills required to perform their tasks.

- Executive and management training in such subjects as new technologies, management systems, communication, leadership, organization, etc.; and ISO 9000 training, to explain how management should direct, use, and maintain the quality system.

- Support of individual external training, such as participation in conferences, seminars, or courses.

These are suggested categories only and do not need to be the same as those listed above. Every company must determine for itself what kinds of training it will provide. But the spectrum should be as broad as possible. Section 4.18 requires that the training program shall comprise all levels of personnel.

List the training categories in procedure

The operational procedure dealing with training should list the training categories and the policies guiding identification of training needs in each category. For example, for departmental training the policy can be that each department identifies its own training needs, taking into consideration:

- the education and experience of newly hired personnel and personnel transferred to new assignments;

- introduction of new equipment and processes;

- results of periodical assessments of personnel; and

- occurrences of product nonconformities and quality system noncompliances.

Documenting general policy guidelines for identification of training needs is sufficient to satisfy the first requirement of Section 4.18. The operational procedure describing the training system does not need to be more

Document general training policy guidelines

specific in this regard. But some companies may want to add more detailed rules governing the administrative aspects of initiation and approval of training; for example, rules for evaluating of training requests from departments or specific policies for individual participation in external training during working hours. If these rules are very detailed, it is better to issue them in separate procedures.

Although the ISO 9000 standard encourages that training be provided to all levels of personnel without emphasizing any specific groups or functions, there is a well established auditing practice defining the minimum scope of the training program. Auditors expect, as a minimum, the following groups of personnel to be trained:

- Quality control inspectors and engineers, and other personnel carrying out inspections, are expected to be trained in the use of measuring and testing equipment, in inspection and testing techniques, and in application of statistical methods.

- Operators of special processes (see Chapter 10) should be trained in carrying out and/or monitoring these processes.

- All personnel in the organization are expected to be trained in the objectives, use, and maintenance of the quality system.

Periodically examine and certify special skills

Personnel assigned to production and inspection processes that require considerable skills may need to be periodically examined and certified. This can be applicable for such processes as radiographic or ultrasonic inspections, welding, and the operation of forklift trucks. The certification can be conducted by professional associations, certification bodies, or accredited laboratories, or can be provided in-house. In any case, the criteria for certification must be defined either directly in a procedure or by reference to applicable standards.

IN-HOUSE TRAINING

Define and record scope and duration of training

Training can be provided in any form that is deemed be effective and suitable. Many people think of training as classroom lecturing or practicing of skills on models or simulators, and are concerned that implementation of ISO 9000 training requirements will be very costly and disruptive. While these forms of training are often appropriate, on-the-job training and self-study can be used extensively to satisfy the requirements of the standard. Auditors will not object to any forms of training as long as the scope and duration are defined, the qualification of instructors are evidenced, and the training is recorded.

Define training specifications

The scope and depth of training must be either specified in advance or be recorded after completion of training. An entry in an employee training file stating that the employee was trained in computers does not have any meaning unless the scope of this training is specified. Any form of training specification is acceptable. It can be a short outline of the training curriculum, a statement of training objectives, or a copy of the training materials. Specification of training is important for two reasons. One is that without the specification there is no way to tell precisely what knowledge or skills can be expected from the trained person; and the second is that specifications assure continuity and consistency from one training session to another.

Establish file for standard training

The requirement for documenting training content can be best complied with by establishing a file for each type of regularly offered training. The file can contain the description of training, masters of the training materials intended for distribution to trainees, a list of approved instructors, blank forms for recording attendance, and so forth.

When simple on-the-job training is provided to an individual person or a small group, and there is no written curriculum or training material, the content of the training can be documented after its completion. For exam-

Document on-the-job training

ple, when an employee is assigned to carry out visual inspection of small parts moving on a production line, the training for this operation would typically consist of:

- explaining what to look for;
- reviewing samples to define the limits of acceptability;
- demonstrating the inspection techniques; and
- monitoring the employee for the first couple of hours on the new assignment.

To document this training, it is sufficient to write a memo or fill out a form, listing these four elements of the training just as they are stated above. No more detail is needed in this simple case.

Define policy for self-study training

Self-studying is rarely thought of as formal training, even though it is by far the most popular method for learning, especially for managers and engineers. Professional and trade magazines, special reports, and books usually supply most of the information that a company needs to upgrade the knowledge of personnel. To actively support this invaluable source of training, companies should define their policy for purchasing and distributing books and magazines, and formally recognize and encourage self-study.

Document self-study training

Self-study is almost never documented or recorded, and in most cases it does not need to be. But whenever the self-study form of training is used to satisfy an ISO 9000 requirement, it will not be accepted if it is not documented. Self-study is appropriate, for example, when learning how to operate new computer software. When a company decides to install a new database system and nobody has any experience with databases, the company has the option of either sending someone to a database course or assigning a person to learn about databases from books and manuals. The self-study option will often be the most suitable. People that have a general knowledge of computers can usually learn how to operate new software without the help of an instructor.

To sufficiently document this self-study training, a memo can be drafted that specifies the training objectives, contents, the reference materials used, and the number of hours spent. Some auditors may not be willing to recognize self-studying as formal training, and will be more diligent in checking the documentation and training records. To avoid any problems, the process of initiating, documenting, and recording self-study training should be described in a procedure, and the documentation and records should be as complete as possible.

Provide evidence of instructor's qualifications

Auditors often ask about the qualifications of training instructors. Most midsize and smaller companies do not need a formal system for evaluation and approval of instructors. But when asked to present evidence that a specific instructor is qualified, the company should be able to show the proof of education, experience, and training that demonstrate the instructor's qualifications.

Instructor for ISO 9000 orientation must be qualified

A common noncompliance is the lack of evidence that the person assigned to provide the general ISO 9000 orientation course to new employees is qualified. It happens often in companies where the initial ISO 9000 training for existing employees is conducted by the quality assurance manager or a consultant, and then the training materials are passed on to someone in the personnel department to train new employees. If the new instructor is not specifically trained in conducting the course, he or she usually does not know enough about quality systems and ISO 9000 to teach others. Auditors often audit the qualifications of instructors by investigating the ISO 9000 training or the internal auditing training. Auditors are very knowledgeable in this area and can judge the level of a person's qualifications by asking just a few questions.

TRAINING RECORDS

Good training records are crucial

Training records are especially important in demonstrating compliance with ISO 9000 training requirements, because there is usually nothing else that would evidence training. Auditors seldom have the opportunity to witness the training itself. Consequently, the whole training system will be judged on the basis of completeness and organization of the records. It is therefore extremely important that the system for recording training is coherent, comprehensive, and well maintained.

Store and maintain training records

The first issue is the responsibility for maintenance and storage of training records. There are basically two possibilities. One is that all training records, irrespective of how and by whom they were established, are maintained and kept by the personnel department. The second is that each department maintains and stores its own training records. I generally instinctively choose decentralized systems, but in this case the centralized system may be a better choice. In practice, it is extremely difficult to ensure coherence, consistency, and continuity of the training system without central coordination.

Consider centralizing training documentation and records

I do not advocate that the personnel department, or other central organization, be responsible for initiating and conducting departmental training. There should be, however, a central authority responsible for ensuring that the training program is coherent and consistent and above all, that the training documentation and records satisfy the requirements dictated by a companywide policy.

When training documentation and training records are kept by individual departments, auditing the training system can be a frustrating experience. The auditor assigned to audit the training system must crisscross the whole company and deal with a variety of different document formats, record indexing systems, and departmental purposes. It is difficult in these circumstances to present a convincing case that the training system is coherent, and consistent, and well controlled.

Maintain training record file for each individual

A popular method for organizing training records is based on maintaining an individual training record file for each person working in the company. All documents evidencing the employee qualifications can be kept in the file. These can be professional resumes, diplomas, certificates, licenses, and records of in-house training. In addition, training overview cards or computer databases should be established to cross-reference employees and the tasks in which they are trained.

Provide quick access to personnel qualification status

The record-keeping system must allow quick access to determine whether specific employee is qualified in a given task, and vice versa. When walking through the company, auditors often note names of inspectors, welders, or other special process operators, and then ask for the evidence that they are qualified. Some auditors investigate the same aspect in reverse. They may ask, for example, which employees are qualified as welders. In companies where the only records of training are lists of participants in a particular course and there are no individual training record files or cross-reference lists, answering either one of these questions can be difficult. I do not mean to imply that course participant lists should not be established and kept. These are valuable records, especially when the participants sign for their attendance. But, standing alone, they do not give a sufficient overview of the companywide training status.

GRANDFATHERING OF EXISTING EMPLOYEES

Many companies preparing for the ISO 9000 certification add new training requirements to their compulsory training program and find themselves with existing employees that, although performing satisfactorily, have not been formally trained in accordance with the new program. These employees can be grandfathered by their supervisors or bosses.

Qualifications can be certified by written declaration

If, for example, a quality lab technician is responsible for calibrating measuring and test equipment, and has been doing it successfully for one year prior to the introduction of a compulsory training course for this function, he or she should not be required to take the course. Instead, the lab's manager can certify, by a written declaration, that the technician is qualified to calibrate specific kinds of measuring and test equipment.

Certificates must contain same information as training record

The certificates of qualification substitute for specific training records required by the training program. They must therefore contain the same kind of information that would be expected in a training record. The certificate should list the skills in which the certified person is judged to be qualified and substantiate the judgment by referring to experience or other evidence. The grandfathering scheme does not change the training and training record system in any way. Training record files are still required for all employees and the grandfathered skills are included in the cross-reference lists or databases, just as though they were acquired by training.

Skills requiring formal certification cannot be grandfathered

Skills that require formal certification based on an exam or a workmanship sample cannot be grandfathered. Even though an employee is performing satisfactorily, there is no assurance that he or she will be able to pass the specified test. Also, grandfathering cannot substitute for such training as general product orientation or introduction to the ISO 9000 quality system. The fact that an employee has been with the company for a long time and is fully qualified in a function does not ensure that he or she knows equally well all company products and the environment in which they work. The same reasoning applies to all other kinds of companywide training, including quality system training.

ISO 9000 TRAINING

Train personnel in understanding and using quality system

Prior to the certification audit, all personnel should be trained in understanding and using the quality system. There is no statement in ISO 9000 that directly requires general quality training, but the auditing practice is firmly established in this regard. Auditors do not believe it is possible to effectively implement and operate a quality system without all personnel knowing how it works. ISO 9004 supports this interpretation. Section 18 contains specific requirements for quality training.

The following issues are usually included in the general quality training:

Sample of topics for ISO 9000 training

- ISO 9000 standards: A short explanation of the ISO 9000 standards, how they are structured, and their application.

- ISO 9000 certification: Explanation of the certification schemes and registrars, and outline of the certification process and maintenance of certification.

- Reasons for implementation of ISO 9000: Discussion of the need for quality management, commercial advantages on international and domestic markets, and anticipated reduction of customer audits.

- ISO 9000 requirements: General overview of all ISO 9000 requirements and discussion of the overall scope of the quality system.

- Quality system elements and objectives: Discussion of the key elements of the quality system, such as the documentation system, internal audits and corrective actions; and explanation of how the quality system works to prevent nonconformities and improve the quality of products.

- Companywide participation: Motivation of personnel to participate in the maintenance and improvement of the quality system, and explanation of specific ways to do it.

When the general quality training is provided just prior to the certification audit, the training should also instruct personnel on how to prepare for and receive the audit. The relevant topics are:

- Explanation of what happens during the certification audit.

- Discussion of the techniques that the auditors use —where they look, how they examine records, what questions they ask, and so forth.

- Instructions for how all employees should prepare themselves and their immediate surroundings for the audit — check documents and records, organize and clean up, and prepare to answer questions.

Training can be classroom, on-the-job, or self-study

The general quality training can take any form deemed by the company to be appropriate and effective. It can be classroom lecturing, on-the-job discussions in small groups, or distribution of written material for self-reading. Auditors will never question the training format and techniques as long as the training content is documented and the training is conducted by a qualified instructor.

Self-study book for ISO 9000 orientation

I have written a 38-page booklet entitled *ISO 9000 In Your Company, Self-study Course for Personnel* (published by AQA Co.). The booklet contains training material on all the topics listed above, with special emphasis on preparing personnel for the certification audit. If the self-study format is chosen for general quality training, and this booklet or any other materials are distributed for reading, all those that receive the materials should sign for them to establish the training record. One copy of the materials themselves can be retained to document the training content.

Train personnel in quality system procedures

In addition to the general ISO 9000 orientation, personnel should be also trained in the use of specific quality system procedures, forms, and techniques that are applicable to their functions. This training usually takes place within the work areas, and it should be provided by supervisors or departmental managers.

15 DOCUMENTS AND RECORDS

Every chapter and section of this book discusses the establishment and maintenance of documents. In particular, Chapter 5, Design Department, includes a section on control of drawings and specifications, and Chapter 10, Production Departments, includes some tips on how to issue and control work instructions. This chapter will discuss document and record control as a companywide system. Even though in many companies individual departments issue and maintain their own documents and records, the classification of documents and the general rules for controlling them should be governed by a companywide policy.

Documents and records concern every department in company

The importance of a well-designed and implemented document control system cannot be overstated. Documents are established in every department and they are used in connection with nearly every activity regulated by the quality system. The results of most activities must also be recorded. The widespread use of documents and records significantly increases the risk that a document or record control noncompliance will be committed and found.

Noncompliances are easy to find

These noncompliances are easy to identify and report. It does not take much auditing experience to note that a document is not authorized or a record is incomplete. Such observations cannot be challenged or discussed. A deficient document is the proof of its own deficiency. Many auditors, especially the less experienced ones, like the simplicity of dealing with the document control related noncompliances and write them up without hesitation.

Classify documents, write and distribute document control procedure, and implement the system

The widespread use of documents and the ease of identifying a deficient document make the document and record control system the most vulnerable during the certification audit. Very special attention should be paid to the design, implementation, and management of this system. The first step is to define and classify all the controlled documents and establish the rules for controlling each category. Then, procedures for the document control system should be written and distributed to every area in the company, and the individual departments should verify that their documents and their document control systems satisfy the new requirements. Finally, after the departments implement the necessary corrections, quality assurance should thoroughly verify compliance in every area of the company.

The requirements pertaining to establishment, issue, and management of documents are stated in ISO 9000 Section 4.5, Document and data control. The section identifies five specific requirements:

- Original issues of documents and document changes, corrections, and revisions must be reviewed and approved prior to release.

- Documents must be distributed to locations where they are used, and their distribution must be defined and/or recorded.

- At distribution, document changes must be summarized, highlighted, or otherwise identified.

- There must be a system — a master list or equivalent — to identify current revision status of documents.

- Obsolete documents must be removed from points of use and, if masters are retained for preservation of knowledge or other purpose, they must be identified and segregated.

Before I discuss the implementation of specific document and record control requirements, I want to discuss the difference between a document and a record. Neither ISO 9001 nor 9002 offers any definition. Sections

**Document
vs
record**

17.2 and 17.3 of ISO 9004, however, are somewhat more helpful by providing examples of the types of documents and the types of records requiring control. Looking at these lists we can see that a document can be defined as an instruction or plan containing information on how a company functions, how specific tasks are to be carried out, and how to build specific products or provide services. A record, by contrast, is a written statement of data and facts pertaining to a specific event, person, process, product, and so forth.

**Form =
document**

**Data recorded
in form = record**

There is not always a clear physical distinction between a document and a record. For example, a form used in an inspection report is a document. It instructs in the scope of the inspection and specifies which data must be recorded. However, once the form is filled out, it becomes a record, a written statement of facts pertaining to a specific event — an inspection that took place at a specific date, time, and location.

SCOPE AND STRUCTURE OF DOCUMENTATION

**ISO 9000 does
not impose spe-
cific structure**

The original edition of the ISO 9000 standards did not specify how the quality system documentation should be structured. The 1994 revision is somewhat more specific, but still does not impose any particular structure. ISO 9000 Section 4.2.1 just mentions that the outline structure of the documentation shall be defined in the quality manual, and that the manual shall include or reference the procedures that form part of the quality system. Otherwise, nearly all sections of the standard contain such phrases as "the supplier shall establish and maintain procedures for . . ." or " the supplier shall document . . .", but there is no mention of the organization or format of the required documentation.

**Customary
organization
and format
not mandatory**

It follows, therefore, that the customary classifications, organization, and formatting of documents that are often recommended by consultants are not mandatory. When addressing special situations or contemplating implementation of unorthodox solutions, it is important to remember that there are no restrictions on the style and format. The broad interpretation of what can be admitted as documentation also helps when handwritten memos, posted signs, equipment manufacturer's manuals, and other non-procedure-like documents are presented to auditors as evidence of compliance with the documentation requirements.

Most companies do not have any reason to experiment and will follow the well-established practice of dividing their quality system documentation into the three classic levels: quality manual, operational procedures, and general work instructions and process procedures.

**Three tiers:
Quality manual
Procedures
Instructions**

In addition to these three groups of documents defining the quality system, the document control requirements also apply to documents defining products and the manner of their production (for example, codes and standards, drawings and specifications, production plans, product-specific instructions and process procedures, and quality plans). Although the method for control are basically the same for both the quality system and the product-specific instructions and process procedures, they will be easier to control if documented separately. The product-specific documents define products, not the quality system, and should not therefore be referred to as either the third or the fourth level of documentation.

**Top level:
Quality manual**

In the traditional three-level structure of quality system documentation, the quality manual is the top level document. The role of the quality manual is to define the policies and outline the company quality system. The manual defines the scope and the elements of the quality system, assigns personnel with authorities and responsibilities necessary to operate the system, provides outlines of major subsystems and procedures, and references operational procedures that govern the application of individual quality system elements.

It is customary to divide the quality manual into the same 20 sections that organize the ISO 9000 standard. It is the best way to ensure that nothing is missed. This organization is also "auditor friendly", as it helps auditors quickly verify whether the documentation complies with the ISO 9000 standard. If the manual is structured in any other way — for example, according to departments or functions — it should be cross-referenced with the 20 sections of the standard.

2nd level: Operational procedures

The second level of the quality system documentation contains the operational procedures. They define systems, provide instructions, and assign authorities and responsibilities for carrying out all the main activities in the quality system. These procedures are also sometimes called system procedures. Normally there should be at least one operational procedure for each element of the quality system, unless the element is not relevant or has been fully defined in the quality manual.

3rd level: Work instructions and process procedures

The third level of the quality system documentation contains the work instructions and process procedures. I include only those instructions that support the quality system, and distinguish them from those that pertain to manufacturing of a specific product or group of products. For example, calibrating a micrometer, operating a computer program or machine, and general painting or welding, are tasks and processes that the company carries out irrespective of which specific product is being manufactured at the time. On the other hand, when special processes, tools, inspection techniques, gauges, handling methods, or packaging are designed for a specific product, and their design is a part of the product design output, the instructions and process procedures are product-specific.

Distinguish between quality system and product-related instructions

This distinction is not important for compliance with ISO 9000, but it helps to efficiently manage the document control system. While the general instructions can be issued and controlled by the departments that use them, the control of product-specific instructions must be tied in with the control of the documents that define the products. With a separate system for product specific-instructions, their scope of application and the responsibility for their establishment and control are unmistakable. It is also possible to identify and control them by the same part or product numbers and revision levels as drawings and specifications. However, many people do not make this distinction and consider the product-specific documents to be third-level documents. It really does not matter as long as they are able to properly reference and control the documentation.

Comprehensive examples of the first two levels of documentation for a quality system can be found in one of my other books, *ISO 9000 Documentation, A 20-section quality manual and 26 operational procedures.*

REVIEW AND APPROVAL OF DOCUMENTS

Establish evidence of review by authorizing signature

The first document control requirement is the review and approval of documents prior to issue. This is usually satisfied by an authorizing signature on the document. The signature signifies that the document was reviewed for correctness and consistency with general policies, and that it is officially authorized for use. When several managers are involved in the review and approval of a document, or the functions of review and authorization are separate, the document may be signed by more than one person.

Predetermine authorization requirements and identify significance of signatures

Deciding how many authorizing signatures are required on any given document should be made internally by the company. ISO 9000 is completely indifferent in this regard and only requires that the authorization requirements be determined in advance. A procedure that contains five boxes for authorizing signatures and is released with only three signed off is not acceptable. If the other two are not relevant for this procedure, they should not exist, or be at least crossed out. Otherwise it is not possible to determine if the authorization process is completed, and if the procedure is formally released for use.

The significance of signatures on documents should be clearly identified, unless only one signature is required and can be assumed to be the sign-off for both the review and authorization. The most common method is appropriate labeling of the signature boxes or using REVIEWED BY:, APPROVED BY:, or AUTHORIZED BY: stamps.

Alternative methods acceptable if there is evidence of review and approval

Some documents, such as parts lists, bills of materials, work orders, or even drawings are established and maintained on computer databases, word processors, or CAD systems, and do not have hard copy masters that can be signed. Auditors are very open to accept alternative methods of identifying the review and approval status of documents in electronic media. But whatever method is used, there must be a record evidencing that a document that can be viewed on either a computer monitor or be printed out has been reviewed and approved. When practicable, the documents should identify the approving authority by name or initials. Other acceptable techniques are keeping logs or hard copies with original authorizing signatures, or signing off directly on labels of read-only protected diskettes. Data bases can be authorized by either approving every addition or change, or by periodical review of the correctness and integrity of data.

Control master disks or backup tapes if electronic media is used

When documents and records are stored in electronic media, auditors will investigate how the master disks and backup tapes are controlled. The requirements are the same as for hard copy master documents. Auditors will expect that the disks are stored in designated locations, they are clearly labeled, and their contents are well organized and identified; and that the system for backing up data identifies who is responsible for the backup, how often is it done, and where the backup tapes are kept.

Auditing the control of documents stored in electronic media is more difficult. Mismanagement of data and files is not visually apparent and it can only be determined by browsing through hard disks, diskettes, and tapes. But auditors normally do not do that. The audit will usually concentrate on the visible and easily auditable elements of the system, such as procedures, storage of disks, and backup of data.

Document and implement system for electronic media documents

Companies that keep most of their documents in the traditional paper media but also have some stored in computers often forget to describe, and even implement, the system for controlling the electronic media documents. Many people have the perception that when a document is stored in a computer it must be correct and it cannot be mixed up with other documents. But a disk or a tape is just a medium that substitutes paper, and it can be just as disorganized as any desk or filing cabinet. When there are any controlled documents stored in the electronic media, the system for controlling these documents should be described in a procedure with the same degree of detail as would be deemed appropriate for paper documents.

DOCUMENT DISTRIBUTION AND REVISION CONTROL

Identify and control the distribution

The requirement for identifying the distribution of documents ties in closely with the requirement for removal of obsolete documents from points of use. The underlying concern is that if it is not known where documents are used, it is not possible to remove them and substitute new revisions. Implementation of these requirements is relatively simple for the quality manual, operational procedures, general work instructions, and other documents that do not change very often and have a well-defined permanent distribution. But it is not always obvious for product-related documentation.

Auditors will test the distribution list

The first three levels of the quality system documentation are usually distributed to predetermined locations and managers. When the distribution list is permanent, it can be printed directly on the documents. An alternative method is to make a record of every distribution and keep it together with the master documents. It can be a distribution cover sheet, a distribution card, or a log. Auditors will test the distribution control system by picking out a couple of procedures and asking where else the procedures are used. They may also go to the indicated locations to check if the procedures are there and ask locally how and when they were delivered.

Two methods for handling obsolete documents

The removal of obsolete documents from points of use can be accomplished by either requesting the return of the old document when the new revision is delivered, or by requiring that the old document be destroyed when it is superseded by a new revision. The first alternative is, of course, more effective and auditors will prefer it. But it requires that new revisions of documents are delivered by hand and that old documents are collected and accounted for. If this seems too much of a burden, the second alternative can be implemented. To reinforce the requirement that the old documents must be destroyed, the new distribution can be accompanied with a note stating, REMOVE AND DESTROY THE DOCUMENTS SUPERSEDED BY THE CURRENT REVISION.

Control product-specific documents

Distribution control of documentation defining products and the manner of their manufacturing can be much more difficult. The interest in these documents is much more widespread, and it cannot be predicted in advance who and when will be using them. But they must be controlled effectively, especially when they are used in production and inspection.

Enclose documents with work orders or establish document stations in work areas

There are two generic models for controlling product-related documents in production and inspection areas. One is to enclose the documents with a work order and destroy them after the production and inspection cycles for that order are completed. The other is to establish document stations at various work areas containing current drawings, specifications, and procedures, and to continuously update the document stations with new document revisions. The first method is applicable in companies manufacturing mostly custom products, and the second method is most suitable when the production is constant. Companies that basically have a constant production but often customize their products can design their control system using elements from both methods.

Avoid unofficial storage of documents

Unofficial storage of documents in production and inspection areas should be prohibited. People often like to have their own private reference files with drawings and specifications retained for no apparent reason. When auditors ask about these files, they are usually told that these are private documents and that they are not used in production.

Some auditors may overlook these private files, but there are also those (including myself) who will ask what these documents are used for and start pulling out their notebooks. Whatever answer is given, it is likely to be a noncompliance. There is no legitimate reason for having private files in the production and inspection areas. Auditors are not only concerned about how documents are used at the time of the audit, but also with the controls to preclude the use of unauthorized or obsolete documents at any time.

Control product-related documents in office area

While control of product-related documents in production and inspection areas can be difficult, many companies do not even pretend to control these documents in the office areas. There is usually no formal distribution system and anyone is free to make copies of documents as needed. In Chapter 5, Design Department, this problem was discussed in the section dealing with reference materials. Designers have a legitimate need to store preliminary and historical documents for reference. But there is no excuse for private reference files in production planning, purchasing, or sales departments. Work orders, purchase orders, and contracts must be established on the basis of authorized and current documents.

Avoid unrestricted self-service access to masters

Companies that would like to retain flexibility to allow office personnel free access to copy documents on an as-needed basis can still do it. They must, however, set up a system assuring that the accessible documents are on the current revision level and are authorized, and that the documents are either destroyed or returned after use if they are not consumed. Allowing unrestricted self-service access to masters may not be a good idea. This will expose the masters to increased risk of being damaged or lost.

Establish file for reproducible copies

For this purpose, it is better to establish a file of reproducible copies and appoint someone to update this file when new revisions are issued. Personnel using this file should be instructed, by posted signs and/or by training, in procedures stating that collecting documents in private files is prohibited. Every copy of a document must be destroyed or returned after use, unless it is marked up and retained as a record, sent out to a vendor or a customer, or is otherwise consumed.

Establish master list for documents and their revision status

ISO 9000 Section 4.5.2 explicitly requires that there must be a master list or equivalent system for identifying the current revision status of documents. Auditors will test the system by pulling a controlled document and asking for confirmation of its revision. A system for revision control of engineering documents was discussed in Chapter 5, and some tips on how to establish a master list for work instructions were given in Chapter 10.

List document name, revision, and approving authority

Generally, it is most efficient to have every department or other organizational unit issuing documents maintaining its own list or log of issued documents. The list should identify each document by a name and/or code number, and indicate its current revision. In addition, the list may identify the person that approved the document and the permanent placement or distribution of copies, unless this is done by another means. Computer databases, manual logs, and document catalog cards are the most popular means of maintaining a revision status master list.

Control revisions in remote locations

Compliance with the requirements for revision status control may be difficult to achieve when documents are not used in the same location where they were established. Typical examples are satellite production plants receiving drawings from headquarters, companies receiving drawings from customers or subcontracted designers, and construction yards. In these cases, it is not sufficient that drawings are logged as they are received. If a new revision was not sent or has been lost in the mail, this would not be known.

196 ISO 9000 QUALITY SYSTEM

To satisfy ISO 9000, either the master list of drawings must be regularly received at the locations where the drawings are used, or there must be a well-defined communication link for checking the revision status of documents. Calling up headquarters and asking for revision status of a document is an acceptable method, provided that it is officially sanctioned and is explained in a procedure. Auditors will not fail to check if the method works satisfactorily.

DOCUMENT CHANGES

Most companies have well-established systems for processing engineering change requests, as discussed in Chapter 5, Design Department. With the introduction of ISO 9000, equivalent systems must be established for requesting changes in all other types of controlled documents. Every department issuing documents can designate its own channels and procedures for processing document change requests.

Establish a system for changing procedures and instructions

Auditors will pay special attention to the mechanisms employed for changing operational procedures and work instructions. A quality system cannot develop and improve without active input from personnel at all levels. Personnel should be formally encouraged to critically review the procedures that affect their work and be instructed how to request changes. At the time of the initial implementation of the quality system, most of the operational procedures are usually established centrally by quality assurance, and they are far from perfect. If within the first couple of months there are no requests to change these procedures, it is a sure sign that nobody cares about the new quality system.

Review and approve changes

Changed or corrected documents must be reviewed and approved by the same authority that issued the original documents, unless designated otherwise. When changes are made by reissue of a document on a higher revision level, the review and approval system can be the same as applied for the initial issue of the document. Reissues are rarely cited with a noncompliance related to their review and approval. The real problem is with handwritten, or so-called red-line, corrections.

Sign-off on red line changes

Anything crossed out, added, or corrected in a controlled document is a noncompliance, unless the change is signed off or initialed by an authorized person. Normally, the authorization should come from the same function that initially approved the document. But there are situations when this is not practical or even feasible. For example, when a minor change is made in a document that was initially approved by five managers, it may not be practical to require the same five managers to approve the change. Or when a drawing needs to be corrected in the field, the engineer that initially approved it may not be available to approve the correction. To account for such situations, the procedure regulating document changes should allow for provisional authorization of red-line corrections. In principle, if such corrections are allowed, they should be approved immediately by the highest competent authority available and be promptly reported to the party that initially issued the document with a request to confirm the authorization for change and/or to reissue the document.

Describe the nature of the change

ISO 9000 Section 4.5.3, Document changes, explicitly requires that: "Where practicable, the nature of the change should be identified in the document or the appropriate attachments". It cannot be expected that those who receive revised documents engage in a systematic comparative analysis of the new and the old document to detect the changes. This is obvious, and most companies do highlight changes at distribution of revised documents, but few have a formal policy and procedures requiring it.

Summarize change on distribution sheet or on document

The words "where practicable" should not be interpreted as "where convenient". Auditors will expect that changes are identified whenever the absence of identification could cause anyone to miss a change. The most common way to identify changes is to summarize them on the distribution cover sheet if one is used. Less formal methods — for example, highlighting, marking on margins, or identifying changes on self-stick notes — are also acceptable, but they must be officially sanctioned in a procedure.

OTHER DOCUMENTS

There are three types of documents that have not been discussed in the preceding sections:

- Copies of current controlled documents that will not be followed up with revisions (often called uncontrolled documents);

- Obsolete revisions of controlled documents; and

- Archives and other documents that are not included in the document control system.

Clearly identify uncontrolled copies

Every company needs to issue copies of controlled documents that will not be kept current (for example, a copy of the quality manual or inspection procedures sent to a customer, or drawings sent to a bank for evaluation of a project). Internal departments of the company may also need uncontrolled documents. For example, the legal department may need copies of inspection procedures to defend a product liability case. The most common way to identify documents that will not be kept current is to stamp them UNCONTROLLED COPY.

In principle, uncontrolled copies of a document may be given only to those internal functions or outside parties who do not manage, perform, or verify work that can be directly affected by the document. It is not acceptable, for instance, that uncontrolled drawings be present in production or inspection areas. All documents sent to a subcontractor must be controlled.

Destroy or clearly identify and segregate obsolete documents

Obsolete revisions of documents normally should be destroyed. But many companies want to retain at least one copy for preservation of knowledge or legal reasons. These documents must be clearly identified and be stored separately from the current documents. The most common way to identify their status is to stamp them OBSOLETE or HISTORY. While identification of obsolete documents is explicitly required in the standard, separation is not. However, I have seen noncompliances identified for lack of separation. Auditors can argue that intermingling obsolete and current documents creates increased risk of unintended use of the obsolete documents, even when they are identified.

Old revisions of documents are acceptable in the servicing department

A special problem arises when old revisions of documents have a legitimate use in servicing or production of spare parts. I personally do not see a problem with storing several revisions of the same drawing together in the servicing area, but would object to such practice in production and inspection, where the overwhelming majority of parts are manufactured and inspected to new drawings. When, occasionally, old parts are manufactured, they can be run as a custom order and the appropriate documentation be attached to the order.

The last category of documents that has not been discussed is all the documents that are not included in the document control system. Some of them are clearly outside of the scope of ISO 9000 and auditors will not touch them. They are financial, legal, commercial, and personnel documents (other than those related to personnel qualifications and training). But there are also many documents, especially technical, that are in the gray area. Examples include drawings of special machines and tools, documentation for products that are no longer manufactured, old files taken over from merged companies, personal files on engineers that no longer work in the company, and so forth. It is incredible how much of these types of documents are stored in some companies.

Archives do not need to be controlled, but must be identified and segregated

While auditors accept in principle the existence of uncontrolled archives, they become impatient when the archives are completely unorganized and are intermingled with current documentation. Auditors often stop in front of filing cabinets and ask if they can see what is in them. When three out of four cabinets contain unidentified and unorganized documents that are either archives or someone's private files, auditors lose confidence in the company's commitment to control documents. Additionally, if the cabinets are mislabeled or are not labeled at all, and there are controlled and uncontrolled documents in the same drawers, auditors are sure to start writing up noncompliances.

Whenever possible, archived documents that do not have any current use should be stored in separate locations designated for this purpose. The area and the cabinets containing such documents should be clearly identified as archives and, if possible, be locked. The principle is the same as applies to quarantine areas for unidentified or nonconforming products. The existence of archives and other types of uncontrolled technical documents should be acknowledged in a procedure. The procedure should explain how cabinets containing archived documents are identified and what measures are employed to restrict access.

CONTROL OF QUALITY RECORDS

One third of audit spent reviewing records

During the certification audit, auditors spend at least one third of their time reviewing records. Records are often the only evidence that some activities take place. Auditors never have the opportunity to participate in a management review meeting or an internal audit, and seldom have the time to observe any activity from start to completion. Records are the principle source of information about the implementation and performance of a quality system. To auditors, if something is not recorded, it did not happen. It is not possible to pass the certification audit with incomplete and poorly organized records.

The requirements pertaining to establishment and management of records are stated in ISO 9000 Section 4.16, Control of quality records. The principal requirements are:

- Records must be established and maintained in compliance with documented procedures;
- Records must be stored properly and be readily retrievable; and,
- Retention periods of records must be specified.

Determine what constitutes a record of the activity

To satisfy the first requirement, the procedures and work instructions regulating individual activities should always state which records must be established at the completion of the activity. It is a good idea to include in every procedure a RECORDS heading and list the required records under this heading. If forms are used for establishing records, the forms should be enclosed in appropriate procedures, and thereby be controlled together with the procedures.

Records can be minutes, memos, electronic media ...

Not all records are established using a form. Minutes of meetings, memoranda, and reports are more suitable for recording conclusions of events like management reviews, design reviews, or qualifications of processes. Some records do not need to be independent documents. Stamping or signing off a purchase order is a perfectly acceptable record of receiving inspection. Electronic media, especially data bases, are also suitable for many types of records.

Describe the format and content required for the record

The procedures and work instructions that call for establishment of a record should explain the format and the manner of establishing it. The content of a record can be defined by a checklist, preprinted form, or general instructions for what information should be included in the record. At a minimum, every record must identify the object, person, or event to which it pertains, must be dated, and must identify the person or function that established the record.

Control the content of record forms

The most common noncompliances are the lack of control of the record forms, different formats and scopes of records pertaining to the same kind of event, and incomplete records. The format of the record forms is not a big issue. Auditors pay more attention to changes in the scope of information required by the forms. If the scope is changed without authorization, it is a document control noncompliance.

Do not leave blanks on forms

Auditors assume that the fields on a record form define the scope of information required to establish the corresponding record. Therefore, if any of the fields are not filled out, they consider the record to be incomplete. This is not always fair, because many forms are not meant to be filled out completely. Different fields may be applicable only to some specific products or situations. If this is the case, it is best to cross out these fields or enter NA (not applicable) when filling out such forms.

Provide easy access to records

Retrievability of records is crucial. Auditors will be asking for records at random and paying attention to how long it takes to retrieve a record. If it happens that a record cannot be found immediately, it is best to tell the auditor right away that there will be a delay in retrieving the record. Encourage him or her to continue with the audit in the meantime. There is nothing more counterproductive to both general impression and morale than having the auditor watch managers and secretaries frantically searching for a record. Although it can be quite entertaining — for the auditor.

Identify retention period

ISO 9000 Section 4.16 explicitly states that retention periods of quality records shall be established and documented in a procedure. Determination of how long to retain a record is usually based on expected life of the concerned product, the length of the warranty period, contractual or legal requirements, and so forth. To implement this requirement, it is sufficient to list all records in a procedure and designate a retention period for each.

16 QUALITY ASSURANCE

When internal auditing and corrective actions do not function properly, the quality system dies

In this last chapter of the book I will talk about the two most important quality system elements: internal auditing, and corrective and preventive actions. The objective of internal auditing is to find out if the quality system is implemented and if it is effective. The objective of corrective actions is to improve the quality system and the processes used for design, manufacturing, and servicing of products. From this statement of objectives alone, the importance of these elements should be evident. When internal auditing and corrective actions do not function properly and effectively, the quality system dies.

Auditors know this and take noncompliances in those areas very seriously. I personally always like to start the certification audit in the quality assurance department and investigate the systems for internal auditing and corrective actions first. These two elements tell the whole story about a company's understanding of and commitment to the quality system. For me it is important to find out early on who am I dealing with and conduct the rest of my audit accordingly. But, fortunately for many auditees, this is not the common approach. To the contrary, many registrars schedule the quality department at the end of the audit. The rationale is that auditors should know the quality system before evaluating the functions that manage it.

INTERNAL VERSUS THIRD-PARTY AUDIT

There are many misconceptions about internal quality audits. Most companies preparing for ISO 9000 certification have never had a formal internal auditing system

Internal audit should verify effectiveness of quality system

and are learning from the beginning. The auditing courses, books, and articles about auditing, and even advice from consultants are usually applicable only to third-party audits. Literal application of third-party audit techniques in internal auditing does not make any sense and can lead to ridiculous situations. Although in theory both internal and external audits have the same objectives — to determine if the quality system complies with the ISO 9000 standard, if it is implemented, and if it is effective — in practice the emphasis is different. The third-party audit focuses on compliance with the standard and implementation, while the internal audit is best suited to verify effectiveness.

Checklists differ for internal and third party audits

When conducting certification audits, I often see internal auditing procedures containing permanent audit checklists for auditors. The first question on most checklists is, "Is the quality policy defined in the corporate quality manual?" There are also such questions as, "In which department are contract reviews made?" or "Is the retention period of quality records established by a written procedure?" These questions are appropriate for a registrar conducting the desk study of a quality manual, but they do not add any value to an internal audit.

Internal determines effectiveness — third party determines compliance

Internal auditors usually know their company and the quality system documentation very well. Their task is not to determine if procedures exist or if their contents comply with ISO 9000, but to determine if the procedures are complete, relevant, and helpful, and if they are consistently applied. The issue is not if the quality policy is defined, but if it is well understood and it motivates the personnel. It is not enough to determine that contract reviews are carried out; the internal auditor should determine if the benefits of contract review justify the time and paper consumed for conducting the reviews. Establishment of retention periods for quality records is one thing, but is the basis for establishing the retention periods rational? Third-party auditors cannot verify these things because they do not know the company they audit and do not have enough time to conduct in-depth investigations of effectiveness. This is where the internal auditor has the advantage and it should not be wasted.

Internal audits can assess effectiveness of processes

Another profound difference between internal and external audits is in the area of process control. Third-party auditors do not audit individual processes or products. The certification audit is limited to comprise only verification of the overall system, assuring adequate process control. But the internal auditors are free to expand the scope of the audit to include assessment of individual processes. They have the time and resources to measure the actual process and product characteristics.

Internal audits are a constructive review of the quality system and performance

Thus, the internal audit and the certification audit are two different events with somewhat different objectives, and the internal auditor needs somewhat different skills than the third-party auditor. Instead of knowing the standard, he needs to know the company and its policies. Instead of understanding body language, she has to understand the technology and processes being audited. Instead of knowing how to ask questions to find out where the problems may be, he should know where the problems are and find out what is being done to deal with them. Internal audits should not be a game of hide and seek, as the third-party audit often is. Rather, it should be a constructive review of the quality system and its performance.

Internal audit can be a valuable tool

I know from my own experience as an auditor that most companies operating an ISO 9000 quality system do not know how to use internal auditing to their advantage. It is immediately evident from their procedures. But this does not prevent them from passing the certification audit and, in fact, many will never find out that they are not doing it right. The certification auditors are not consultants and they usually do not comment on what they see as long as ISO 9000 is complied with. They just verify that internal audits are planned, auditors are independent, and the results of the audits are reported and followed up.

INTERNAL AUDIT PLAN

Plan and schedule the audit

A plan and a schedule of the internal audit cycle are indispensable to complying with ISO 9000. Section 4.17, Internal quality audits, explicitly requires planning and scheduling. To complete an audit cycle, every element of the quality system must be audited at least once in all areas where it is implemented. The maximum acceptable period for an audit cycle is one year, which is usually sufficient for fully mature quality systems. Newly implemented systems should be audited more frequently. In the maturation phase — typically the first two years — the audit cycle can be set at six months or less. A six-month cycle has the additional advantage of coinciding with the periodicity of the certification surveillance audits. When the two cycles are synchronized, the internal auditing can be used to prepare the company for the certification surveillance audits.

Conduct first internal audit before certification audit

The first internal auditing cycle must be completed before the initial certification audit. Most registrars do not certify quality systems that have not been audited internally. Without completing the internal auditing cycle there can be no confidence that the quality system is ready for certification. When preparing for the ISO 9000 certification, it is best to start the internal auditing about two months before the certification audit, and complete this first cycle within a month or less. The remaining month will allow time to rectify the residual problems identified by the internal audits.

Audit can be distributed over audit cycle period

The internal auditing can be either distributed over the whole period of the auditing cycle, or be carried out all at once like the certification audit. Nearly all companies choose distributed auditing. Indeed, it is the best choice. Distributed auditing reduces disruption, allows for gradual building of auditing experience, and provides continuing monitoring of the quality system. Internal auditing should not be the kind of shock event as is the certification audit. Over time, it should become a routine activity fully integrated with all other activities in the company.

Determine auditable units using matrix

The smallest auditable unit is a single element of the quality system implemented in a single area or function. To determine how many and which element/areas there are, it is best to make a matrix listing on the vertical side all the elements of the quality system and on the horizontal side all the areas of the company, and associate the areas where each element is applicable.

For example, the element of product identification and traceability is applicable in design (assignment of part numbers), in receiving (identification marking), in storage and production (maintenance of identification), and in shipping (identification marking on packaging). Another example. The element of nonconforming product control is applicable in quality control (identification of nonconforming product), production (maintenance of labeling and segregation), and quality assurance (disposition and preventive action). There are also elements that are applicable in nearly all areas; for example, document control.

Identify quality system elements and relevant company functions

It is customary to use the 20 sections of the ISO 9000 standard to divide the quality system into elements, but the final selection does not need to be the same. Sections that are not applicable of course can be omitted, and sections containing many fairly unrelated requirements (for example, process control) can be further divided into additional elements. Dividing the company into relevant functions and areas usually follows the company's organization, product lines, and physical layout of areas. A typical midsize manufacturing company can be divided into the following areas: management, marketing, sales, design, production planning, purchasing, receiving, storage, several production departments, quality control, packaging, shipping, servicing, personnel, and quality assurance. These are just examples. Every company must determine for itself the areas that are relevant.

On a typical matrix of about 20 quality system elements and 15 areas, there will be somewhere between 50 to 80 element/area units. Quality professionals call these element/area units *quality activities* or, simply, *activities*.

Audit each area and applicable elements vs Audit each element in applicable areas

I will also use this name in the remainder of this chapter. To set up the internal audit plan, the activities must be lumped together into a number of audit blocks. Assuming an audit every two weeks for a period of six months calls for a total of about 25 partial audits. The choice of the activities that will be audited together must be planned carefully. To minimize disruption, it is best to take one area at a time and audit all the applicable elements of the quality system in this area. But to get a good picture of how the system performs, it is better to do just the opposite: take one element at a time and audit it in all areas where it is implemented. The final audit plan will end up being a compromise between these two approaches.

Audit each activity at least once during cycle

Each identified activity must be audited at least once during the internal auditing cycle, regardless of its importance and performance history. This is the baseline requirement. In addition, the ISO 9000 standard also requires that the audits be scheduled on the basis of the status and importance of the activity to be audited. In other words, the frequency of audits should be increased for those activities that are either especially important or have a history of quality problems. Certification auditors do not fail to note if the internal audit plan provides for additional audits of selected activities. If it does not, it strongly indicates that there is no commitment and intent to use the internal auditing effectively, and the audit plan is just another piece of paper to satisfy auditors.

Schedule the audit plan

Once the audit plan is prepared, it should be scheduled over the auditing cycle. It is best to schedule the audits as regularly as possible. If the audits are always conducted every second Tuesday, for example, the auditing will quickly become a routine event, one of company's usual activities. The sequence of auditing different departments and quality system elements is not as important as it is in third-party auditing. For a certification audit, many considerations precede the establishment of the audit plan. The expertise of the individual auditors, the need to gradually learn about how the company works while conducting the audit, the impressions gained during review of the documentation, and so forth: None of these considerations need to be taken into account in internal auditing. The only requirement is that departmental managers be available to assist the auditors.

Matrix constitutes evidence of planning and scheduling

To evidence compliance with the requirement for planning and scheduling the internal audits, it is sufficient to show the certification auditors the matrix identifying the relevant activities and a schedule for the auditing cycle. The matrix is important to demonstrate that all relevant activities are accounted for and none will be missed. The schedule can be in the form of a calendar with audits penciled in under selected dates. Every audit should be identified by naming the quality system elements and areas to be audited and the name of the assigned lead auditor. A sure way to impress the certification auditors is to hang the schedule on the wall behind the quality manager's desk and use it as a tool for coordination of the whole internal auditing program, including follow-up audits.

CONDUCTING INTERNAL AUDITS

Third-party audits are conducted by a team of auditors (assessors) directed by a lead auditor. The size of the team is determined by the consideration of how many auditors are required to complete the audit within three to five days. The third-party audits should be as short as possible to minimize cost and disruption. These considerations are not relevant for internal audits, especially when the audit is distributed over the whole auditing cycle. Thus, as far as capacity is concerned, the internal audits can be conducted by just one person, even in large companies.

Avoid one-person teams

One-person audit teams, however, should be avoided unless the auditor is experienced and has a lot of authority. A team, even a two-person team, carries much more weight. The managers being audited tend to take the audit more seriously when dealing with two persons. Also, auditors tend to be more thorough and hold their ground better when they have the support of a colleague.

Auditors must be independent of activity to be audited

ISO 9000 Section 4.17, Internal quality audits, explicitly requires that internal audits be carried out by personnel independent of those having direct responsibility for the activity being audited. In most companies it is the quality assurance manager that is responsible for conducting the internal audits, and this is a good choice. The quality manager is usually the best qualified and the most motivated person for the job. But when quality assurance functions are audited, someone else must be appointed to conduct the audit.

Encourage companywide participation in auditing

Although it is best when the internal audits are directed by managers with experience and authority, everyone in the company should be invited to participate as support auditors. A volunteer from any department, except the one being audited, could be the second person in the audit team. Opening the audit process to all personnel has an important psychological benefit: it eliminates the negative perception that the audit is another management tool to control personnel. Many companies are sensitive to this issue and avoid assigning any managers at all to the audit team. An all-volunteer audit team may be an excellent motivational tool for galvanizing the interest and commitment of all personnel for the quality system, but they tend to be rather inefficient and often unable to achieve the objectives of the audit.

Auditors must be qualified

Certification auditors always ask about qualifications and training of internal auditors. I personally do not believe that internal auditors must be formally trained and certified. As I argued in the first section of this chapter, internal auditors do not need many of the investigative skills that are indispensable to third-party auditors. Internal auditors should have a good understanding of the objectives of the audit and know how to prepare for the audit as well as how to report its findings.

The best evidence that an auditor is qualified is a certificate from a course for internal auditors. There are

**Best evidence
is internal auditor
certificate**

many auditing courses offered today by universities, professional and industrial associations, registrars, and consultants. When one or two persons in the company are certified by an outside course, they can then organize in-house training for other volunteer auditors who will participate in audit teams.

When a consultant is helping with the implementation of ISO 9000, he or she can also train internal auditors. The scope of training can comprise some four hours of classroom training and a few days of practical training while assisting the consultant in internal auditing. Upon completion of the training, the consultant can issue cer-tificates to the trained personnel. In smaller companies, the certification auditors should accept self-study and self-acquired experiences as sufficient internal auditor training. No matter how the training is acquired, it must be documented and recorded (see Chapter 14, Training).

**Document
how to prepare
for audit in
procedure**

The operational procedure dealing with internal audit-ing should instruct auditors in how to prepare for the audit. They should familiarize themselves with the rel-evant requirements of the ISO 9000 standard, the qual-ity manual, and operational procedures; and review the nonconformity reports, corrective action files, and old audit reports. They should also plan the audit and pre-pare their checklists.

INTERNAL AUDIT REPORT

Third-party audit findings are usually expressed as non-compliances, which are descriptions of conditions, situ-ations, and practices that do not comply with the ISO 9000 standard or with documents defining the products, the manner of production, and the quality system. The advantage of this reporting format is that unsatisfac-tory conditions are clearly and precisely identified, and there is no ambiguity about what needs to be corrected. On the other hand, this format as used by the third-party auditors is not suitable for recording more gen-eral observations concerning the relevance and effec-tiveness of the audited activities.

Irrelevance and ineffectiveness are noncompliances

Internal audits can use the same format of reporting, but the definition of a noncompliance should be broader to include the lack or suspicion of the lack of relevance and effectiveness. For example, certification auditors will never object to an overkill procedure prescribing a complex administrative system to achieve a questionable, or even irrelevant, objective. But internal auditors should not fail to report such a condition, even though it does not violate the ISO 9000 standard.

In such situations there is a temptation to wander from the format of noncompliances, and report conditions of irrelevance or ineffectiveness in the form of narrative observations. The problem with observations is that they are usually judgmental, and could involve the auditor in solution finding. We all know the response, "If you think this is wrong, why don't you tell us how to do it." Another problem is that if the description of an unsatisfactory condition is not phrased as a specific noncompliance, there is no way to immediately activate the system for requesting a corrective action.

State irrelevance or ineffectiveness in simple factual manner

Returning to the example of the complex and questionable procedure, the noncompliance could simply state: Procedure XYZ prescribes complex administrative system with questionable value. In response to this noncompliance, the department that uses and/or established the procedure could propose a corrective action consisting of 1) defining precisely the objectives of the procedure, 2) investigating if there are simpler ways for achieving these objectives, and 3) changing the procedure accordingly. Although the noncompliance is not based on facts (which is unacceptable in a certification audit) but rather on judgment, stating it in a simple and factual manner allows the use of the established corrective action mechanisms.

Recommendation format is not effective

I adamantly defend the audit reporting format based on noncompliances because other formats do not work. The format of recommendations, where auditors request implementation of specific solutions, does not work because it prevents the responsible managers from analyzing the root causes of their problems and proposing their own solutions. The format of long descriptive observations does not work either because, even though it presents the problems with all their complexities, it leads to a dead end. There is no mechanism that automatically initiates a corrective action. The report goes into a drawer and nothing is ever done about it.

Use audit noncompliance reporting format

Following the above arguments, the internal audit reporting system can be very similar to the system used for reporting third-party audits. ISO 9000 certification auditors record every identified noncompliance on a separate form. The form is very similar to that used for corrective action requests and an example (Audit Noncompliance Form) is provided in the *ISO 9000 Documentation* book. It is a one-page form divided into the following four blocks:

- The first block is used for identifying the audit, the area where the noncompliance was noted, and the violated procedure and section of the standard.

- The second block is reserved for describing the noncompliance. The description should precisely identify the object, location, and context of the noncomplying condition, and objectively state the nature of the noncompliance, using concise and factual language. If noncompliances are graded (for example, major and minor) the grade can be identified in this block. At the bottom of the block there are signature boxes for the auditor and the manager responsible for the activity pertaining to the noncompliance. Acknowledgment by the responsible manager helps to avoid any future discussions and attempts to challenge the factual circumstances on which the noncompliance is based.

- The third block is used for proposing the corrective action to address the noncompliance. The block is filled out by the responsible manager. If the root causes of the noncompliance are immediately apparent, the corrective action can be proposed by the completion of the audit. Otherwise, the manager should be given sufficient time to investigate the causes and propose a solution. The block also contains a box for recording the mutually agreed-to due date for implementation of the corrective action and signature boxes for the responsible manager and the auditor.

- The fourth block is reserved for closing out the corrective action. Upon verification that the proposed corrective action is implemented and it is effective, the auditor signs off in this block. If the result of the follow-up audit is unsatisfactory, the auditor can extend the implementation due date.

Compile final audit report

The final audit report does not need to be very elaborate. It can consist of a cover page with the particulars of the audit, and copies of all the individual noncompliance reports established during the audit, using the form discussed above. To provide some statistics and facilitate tracking of corrective action closeouts, the cover page can contain a table listing all noncompliances, due dates for implementation of corrective actions, and fields for recording the status of the corrective actions. If deemed desirable, the report can also include a summary and conclusions from the audit.

When the auditing cycle is completed, the individual audit reports should be bound together into one final report for presentation at the management review meeting. The final report should also contain statistics, conclusions, and recommendations for management. As mentioned earlier in this chapter, companies that do not complete at least one internal auditing cycle, including the issue of a final report and its evaluation by a management review, will usually not be eligible for the certification audit — or risk a major noncompliance and a failed audit.

CORRECTIVE AND PREVENTIVE ACTION

In the new 1994 edition of the ISO 9000 standard, Section 4.14 has a new title and is somewhat expanded and reorganized. The previous title, *Corrective action*, is now

Preventive action added to standard

changed to *Corrective and preventive action;* and accordingly, a new subsection dealing with preventive action is added. Also, an introductory paragraph is added and the text is rearranged. At first it looks like a significant change, but in fact there are no new requirements. While the original 1987 edition of the standard did not use the phrase *preventive action*, it already required elimination of potential causes of nonconformities.

Actual nonconformities vs Potential nonconformities

The distinction between corrective and preventive action is that corrective action deals with actual nonconformities and preventive action deals with potential nonconformities. The only difference in processing a corrective and preventive action is in the first step of identifying the problem that requires attention. All the other steps of the process can be exactly the same for both actions, and there is usually no need to have two independent systems and procedures. In this section I will discuss the corrective and preventive actions together without distinguishing between the two (unless I indicate so explicitly), and will use the phrase corrective action to denote both.

The elements of a corrective action process are:

- Identifying problems that may require a corrective action;
- Deciding if a corrective action is required;
- Correcting the problem (not relevant for preventive actions and not always possible for corrective actions);
- Investigating and determining the root causes of the problem, and proposing appropriate corrective action;
- Implementing the corrective action to eliminate the root causes; and
- Verifying that the corrective action is implemented and that it is effective.

Identification of problems that may require corrective actions should concern everyone in the company. By nature of their functions, process operators, inspectors, and auditors are most active in identifying the prob-

216   ISO 9000 QUALITY SYSTEM

Everyone should be encouraged to be proactive

lems. However, everyone else should be also encouraged to suggest initiation of corrective actions. Initiation of a corrective action can be caused by identification of a major product nonconformity, accumulation of minor nonconformities of a similar character, recurring problem with a process or operation, a noncompliance raised during an audit (internal or external), field performance problems reported by servicing or marketing, customer complaints, nonconforming deliveries from suppliers or subcontractors, and so forth.

Evaluate feasibility of corrective action

A company's capacity to handle and implement corrective actions is limited. Some of them can be very disruptive and costly. The suggestions for corrective actions must be evaluated and approved by the management before they are issued as formal corrective action requests. It is usually the quality manager who decides if a corrective action is required and who issues the formal corrective action requests. However, when the quality manager is directly responsible for the problem that may require correction, someone else should make the decision and issue the corrective action request. The principle is the same as in auditing. The function evaluating the need for corrective action should be independent from the function responsible for the activity where the corrective action will be implemented.

Specifically identify responsibility for corrective action

Corrective action requests should be issued to specific and identified managers, functions, or departments, just as are audit noncompliances. Without clear identification of the authority requesting the corrective action and the party responsible for proposing the solution and implementing it, there will be no accountability and the system will not work.

Record CAR

A very common vehicle for requesting and processing corrective actions is a corrective action request (CAR) form. The form is very similar to that used for recording internal audit noncompliances. An example of such form is provided in the *ISO 9000 Documentation* book. It is a one-page form divided into the following four blocks:

- The first block is used for identifying the party requesting the corrective action (usually the quality manager) and the responsible party receiving the request. Also, the event that triggered the request, such as nonconformity report, customer complaint, etc. is referenced in this block.

- The second block is reserved for describing the unsatisfactory condition that needs to be corrected. There are signature boxes at the bottom of the block for the manager issuing the CAR and the responsible manager receiving it. Acknowledgment by the responsible manager helps to avoid any future discussions and attempts to challenge the factual circumstances on which the CAR is based.

- The third block is used for proposing the corrective and preventive action to address the identified problem. The block is filled out by the responsible manager. If the root causes of the problem are immediately apparent, the corrective action can be proposed at the same time it is requested. Otherwise, the manager should be given sufficient time to investigate the causes and propose a solution. The block also contains a box for recording the mutually agreed-to due date for implementation of the corrective action, as well as signature boxes for the responsible manager and the manager who initiated the CAR.

- The fourth block is reserved for closing out the corrective action. Upon verifying that the proposed corrective action is implemented and is effective, the manager who initially issued the CAR signs off in this block. If the result of the follow-up verification is unsatisfactory, the implementation due date can be extended.

Purchasing issues supplier CARs

Corrective action requests should not only be issued to internal functions or departments but also to suppliers and subcontractors who deliver nonconforming products. The procedure for serving the requests can be identical to that used internally. The only difference may be

218 ISO 9000 QUALITY SYSTEM

that the corrective action requests will be issued by the purchasing department instead of quality assurance. These issues were discussed in Chapter 7, Purchasing Department.

Initiate preventive actions based on anticipated problems

With the new division between corrective and preventive actions introduced in the 1994 revision of ISO 9000, auditors will be asking explicitly for evidence that preventive actions are being implemented. Until now, auditors only required that every corrective action have a preventive element — prevention of recurrence of the problem. A true preventive action is initiated on the basis of anticipated problems rather than their occurrence.

Sources of anticipated problems

The sources of information that can lead to the identification of a need for preventive action are process control records, service reports, minor nonconformity reports, general customer complaints, and other records of quality problems that individually may not warrant initiation of a corrective action, but in aggregate can demonstrate unfavorable trends that must be corrected before they develop into a serious problem. To evidence compliance with ISO 9000 Section 4.14.3, Preventive action, the company must demonstrate that quality records are regularly analyzed to detect unfavorable trends, and show some examples of implementing preventive actions.

A P P E N D I X

The following documents and records will be reviewed by auditors during the ISO 9000 certification audit. Not all of them are directly named in the standards but, when applicable, all will be expected. The documents and records that are explicitly required are identified with an asterisk. The documents listed here are those that are required in addition to the quality manual and operational procedures.

Sect.	Documents	Records
4.1	■ Quality policy * ■ Organizational charts * ■ Appointment of management representative *	■ Management review records *
4.2	■ Quality system manual * ■ Operational procedures * ■ Quality plans *	
4.3	■ Procedures, checklists, or forms with the scope of order/contract review	■ Orders and change orders * ■ Contract review records *
4.4	■ Design project plans and schedules * ■ Design input documents * ■ Codes and standards ■ Design output documents (drawings, specifications, calculations, procedures, etc.) * ■ Bills of materials, material spec sheets, and parts lists ■ Process procedures	■ Design input review records * ■ Design review records * ■ Approvals and authorizations of design output documents * ■ Design verification records * ■ Design validation reports * ■ Design change requests * ■ Serial numbers and configuration records

Sect.	Documents	Records
4.5	■ Master lists of documents * ■ Document distribution lists	■ Approvals and authorizations on issued documents * ■ Document distribution cover sheets and records
4.6	■ Approved subcontractor list * ■ Procedures or checklists with the scope of purchase order/subcontract review	■ Purchase orders and sub-contracts * ■ Subcontractor qualification records * ■ Records of subcontractor performance monitoring * ■ Purchase order/subcontract review records *
4.7	■ Instructions for handling and storage of customer supplied products	■ Records of loss or damage of customer products *
4.8	■ Parts lists ■ Traceability plans	■ Traceability records *
4.9	■ Production plans * ■ Work instructions * ■ Workmanship standards * ■ Process procedures * ■ Process control procedures * ■ Environmental control procedures ■ Production equipment maintenance plan *	■ Production records * ■ Process qualification records ■ Process control records ■ Environmental control monitoring records ■ Production personnel qualification records ■ Production equipment maintenance records *
4.10	■ Inspection and testing program (quality plan) * ■ Inspection checklists (scope) ■ Inspection procedures	■ Inspection and testing records * ■ Inspection personnel qualification records

Sect.	Documents	Records
4.11	■ Measuring equipment inventory and status list * ■ Calibration instructions	■ Calibration records (certificates) *
4.12	There is usually no need for special documents and records	
4.13		■ Nonconforming material and product reports *
4.14		■ Customer complaints and their processing records * ■ Corrective and preventive action requests and reports *
4.15	■ Procedures for special handling methods ■ Procedures for control of environmental conditions ■ Packaging specifications ■ Procedures for special preservation methods ■ Procedures for special loading, protection, and delivery methods	■ Heavy lifting equipment certification ■ Special equipment operator qualification records ■ Stock inventory records * ■ Reports from assessments of product in stock * ■ Environmental control monitoring records
4.16	■ Specification of retention periods for quality records *	
4.17	■ Internal audit plan and schedule *	■ Internal audit reports *
4.18	■ Training program and policies for providing training ■ Documentation of training content and scope *	■ Records of personnel qualifications and training * ■ Instructor qualification records *

Sect.	Documents	Records
4.19	■ Quality plan in servicing (inspections and testing) *	■ Servicing records * ■ Servicing verification records (inspection) *
4.20	■ Statistical process control procedures * ■ Sampling plans *	■ Process control records * ■ Inspection records *

INDEX

Other ISO 9000 Books
by Jack Kanholm

ISO 9000 EXPLAINED
65 Requirements Checklist And Compliance Guide

The book identifies and explains 65 distinct requirements contained in the ISO 9000 standards. Nothing is left out of this complete and exhaustive checklist.

The requirements are phrased in the form of specific actions that need to be taken to ensure compliance. Every requirement is stated in a concise phrase, set in bold type, and is followed with an explanation of the interpretation, procedures, records, and auditing practices relevant to the requirement. Each of these issues is explained under its own heading.

This book is the leading title in the AQA ISO 9000 series. Its role in the series is to introduce the requirements in a systematic manner and explain the basic scope of the actions that must be taken to comply.

ISO 9000 Explained was the first ISO 9000 book published in the USA, and it is still the No. 1 bestseller with over 20,000 copies sold. — AQA Co. 116 pages.

ISO 9000 DOCUMENTATION
A 20-Section Quality Manual and 27 Operational Procedures

This book contains the first two levels of ISO 9001 quality system documentation. The manual and procedures are carefully designed to represent a generic model of a quality system that is simple, natural, and free from excessive paperwork. The strong point of the documentation is

that it defines the baseline — the simplest fully developed system that is certifiable. Nothing in this documentation is superfluous, but what is in there is complete and sufficient.

The book can be used as an illustration to better understand the ISO 9000 standards, as a model for designing and documenting a quality system, or as a ready-made documentation. — AQA Co., 152 pages.

ON COMPUTER DISK WITH COPYRIGHT: Companies that would like to use the text of this book in their quality system documentation can also purchase a copyright permission with a computer disk containing the full text of the book.

ISO 9000 IN YOUR COMPANY
Self-Study Course for Personnel

This booklet contains a list of the ISO 9000 requirements, explains how a quality system works, and instructs employees on how to maintain and improve the quality system. There is also a section explaining how the certification audit is conducted, what questions auditors will ask, and how employees should prepare themselves and their immediate work areas for the audit.

This self-study booklet is intended for distribution to all employees, eliminating the need for costly and disruptive classroom training. It is the most effective way to prepare personnel for implementation of ISO 9000 and the certification audit. — AQA Co., 32 pages.

A quantity-discount version of the booklet is also available for orders of 100 or more.

The books can be ordered directly from AQA Co. by using the form on the reverse side.

ORDER FORM

QNT	PUBLICATION	PRICE	DSCNT	TOTAL
	ISO 9000 Explained - J. Kanholm	$ 49.	%	
	ISO 9000 Documentation - J. Kanholm	$ 88.	%	
	ISO 9000 Quality System - J. Kanholm	$ 98.	%	
	ISO 9000 In Your Company - J. Kanholm	$ 28.	%	
	Q91 (ISO 9001) Standard	$ 15.	NA	
	Q92 (ISO 9002) Standard	$ 15.	NA	
	"ISO 9000 Documentation" text on computer disk and copyright permission	$ 490.	NA	
Add 8.25% sales tax for CA		GRAND TOTAL		

QUANTITY DISCOUNTS

5 to 9 copies: 10%   10 to 19 copies: 20%   20 to 39 copies: 30%   40 to 100 copies: 40%

SHIPPING ADDRESS

Mr. ❑   Ms. ❑ _____

Title _____

Company _____

Street _____

City _____ State _____ Zip _____

Phone & Fax

SHIPPING BY UPS

		USA	CAN
❑	Ground	$ 5.	$ 8.
❑	3rd Day	$ 7.	NA
❑	2nd Day	$ 9.	NA
❑	Next Day	$ 16.	$ 36.
❑	Air Mail to Canada		$ 8.

Shipping of 4 books or more and/or to destinations outside the continental USA will be charged at the actual cost.

BILLING ADDRESS

Company _____

Dept. _____

Street _____

City _____ State _____ Zip _____

Attention

PAYMENT

❑   Check Enclosed
❑   Bill Company
P.O. No.: (Optional)

_____
Sorry, we are not set up to charge credit cards.

Date _____   Signature _____

To order, fax this form to (213) 222 5239, call (213) 222 3600, or mail to AQA Co. — 334 Crane Blvd. — Los Angeles — CA 90065

ISO 9000 QUALITY SYSTEM

Other ISO 9000 Books
by Jack Kanholm

ISO 9000 EXPLAINED
65 Requirements Checklist And Compliance Guide

The book identifies and explains 65 distinct requirements contained in the ISO 9000 standards. Nothing is left out of this complete and exhaustive checklist.

The requirements are phrased in the form of specific actions that need to be taken to ensure compliance. Every requirement is stated in a concise phrase, set in bold type, and is followed with an explanation of the interpretation, procedures, records, and auditing practices relevant to the requirement. Each of these issues is explained under its own heading.

This book is the leading title in the AQA ISO 9000 series. Its role in the series is to introduce the requirements in a systematic manner and explain the basic scope of the actions that must be taken to comply.

ISO 9000 Explained was the first ISO 9000 book published in the USA, and it is still the No. 1 bestseller with over 20,000 copies sold. — AQA Co. 116 pages.

ISO 9000 DOCUMENTATION
A 20-Section Quality Manual and 27 Operational Procedures

This book contains the first two levels of ISO 9001 quality system documentation. The manual and procedures are carefully designed to represent a generic model of a quality system that is simple, natural, and free from excessive paperwork. The strong point of the documentation is that it defines the baseline — the simplest fully developed system that is certifiable. Nothing in this documentation is superfluous, but what is in there is complete and sufficient.

The book can be used as an illustration to better understand the ISO 9000 standards, as a model for designing and documenting a quality system, or as a ready-made documentation. — AQA Co., 152 pages.

ON COMPUTER DISK WITH COPYRIGHT: Companies that would like to use the text of this book in their quality system documentation can also purchase a copyright permission with a computer disk containing the full text of the book.

ISO 9000 IN YOUR COMPANY
Self-Study Course for Personnel

This booklet contains a list of the ISO 9000 requirements, explains how a quality system works, and instructs employees on how to maintain and improve the quality system. There is also a section explaining how the certification audit is conducted, what questions auditors will ask, and how employees should prepare themselves and their immediate work areas for the audit.

This self-study booklet is intended for distribution to all employees, eliminating the need for costly and disruptive classroom training. It is the most effective way to prepare personnel for implementation of ISO 9000 and the certification audit. — AQA Co., 32 pages.

A quantity-discount version of the booklet is also available for orders of 100 or more.

The books can be ordered directly from AQA Co. by using the form on the reverse side.

ORDER FORM

QNT	PUBLICATION	PRICE	DSCNT	TOTAL
	ISO 9000 Explained - J. Kanholm	$ 49.	%	
	ISO 9000 Documentation - J. Kanholm	$ 88.	%	
	ISO 9000 Quality System - J. Kanholm	$ 98.	%	
	ISO 9000 In Your Company - J. Kanholm	$ 28.	%	
	Q91 (ISO 9001) Standard	$ 15.	NA	
	Q92 (ISO 9002) Standard	$ 15.	NA	
	"ISO 9000 Documentation" text on computer disk and copyright permission	$ 490.	NA	
Add 8.25% sales tax for CA		GRAND TOTAL		

QUANTITY DISCOUNTS

5 to 9 copies: 10%   10 to 19 copies: 20%   20 to 39 copies: 30%   40 to 100 copies: 40%

SHIPPING ADDRESS

Mr. ❏   Ms. ❏ _____

Title _____

Company _____

Street _____

City _____ State _____ Zip _____

Phone & Fax _____

SHIPPING BY UPS

		USA	CAN
❏	Ground	$ 5.	$ 8.
❏	3rd Day	$ 7.	NA
❏	2nd Day	$ 9.	NA
❏	Next Day	$ 16.	$ 36.
❏	Air Mail to Canada		$ 8.

Shipping of 4 books or more and/or to destinations outside the continental USA will be charged at the actual cost.

BILLING ADDRESS

Company _____

Dept. _____

Street _____

City _____ State _____ Zip _____

Attention _____

PAYMENT

❏ Check Enclosed
❏ Bill Company

P.O. No.: (Optional)

_____

Sorry, we are not set up to charge credit cards.

Date _____   Signature _____

To order, fax this form to (213) 222 5239, call (213) 222 3600, or mail to AQA Co. — 334 Crane Blvd. — Los Angeles — CA 90065

ISO 9000 QUALITY SYSTEM